THE FOREIGN POLICY OF THE

BRITISH LABOUR GOVERNMENT

1945-1951

INTERNATIONAL STUDIES

of the Committee on International Relations
University of Notre Dame

The Foreign Policy of the British Labour Government: 1945-1951
by M. A. Fitzsimons

Bolshevism: An Introduction to Soviet Communism
by Waldemar Gurian

Christian Democracy in Italy and France
by Mario Einaudi and François Goguel

Europe Between Democracy and Anarchy
by Ferdinand A. Hermens

The Soviet Union: Background, Ideology, Reality
Edited by Waldemar Gurian (Out of Print)

IN PREPARATION

Pan-Slavism
by Hans Kohn

Diplomacy in a Whirlpool: Hungary between Nazi Germany and the Soviet Union
by Stephen Kertesz

The Social Ethic of German Protestantism: 1848-1933
by W. O. Shanahan

The Catholic Church in World Affairs
Edited by Waldemar Gurian and M. A. Fitzsimons

The Foreign Policy Of The British Labour Government 1945-1951

by

M. A. FITZSIMONS

University of Notre Dame Press
Notre Dame, Indiana

PREFACE

"Nobody lets daylight into the corridors of the F. O. [Foreign Office]," wrote T. E. Lawrence to Lord Lloyd. The comment, however, is not wholly true. In the aftermath of each of the two world wars British foreign policy documents have been published for the eager scrutiny of the historian. But on recent events there is no British equivalent of *Speaking Frankly*, or, since the war, of the Council on Foreign Relations annual series, *The United States in World Affairs*. My study is the attempt of an outsider to fill the gap. Not daylight in the Foreign Office, but a lighting up of the major lines and development of British foreign policy, while the Labour Government held office, is my aim.

British foreign policy, unlike that of the Soviet Union, cannot be described in stark bold outlines. It has always been more noted for its adjustments and opportunism than for Grand Designs, for the balance of power was too flexible a policy to be called a Grand Design. In the postwar years, the waning of British power has been a major consideration in the formulation of a foreign policy to advance the world interest of Britain. The task fell to Labour's Foreign Secretary, Ernest Bevin, who through the years conducted an interesting dialogue on the subject with Winston Churchill. Robert Naunton's characterization of Sir Walter Raleigh may fittingly describe the achievement of Bevin, and of British foreign policy in general: "if ever man drew virtue out of necessity, it was he."

In completing this foray of an historian into contemporary affairs, I accumulated many debts. Two in particular call for acknowledgment. The University of Notre Dame generously enabled me to do research in England, and my colleagues on the Committee on International Relations and on the Notre Dame faculty assisted me in many ways.

M. A. Fitzsimons

TABLE OF CONTENTS

CHAPTER ONE

Ideals, Policy and British Power

"Therefore, I say that it is a narrow policy to suppose that this country or that is to be marked out as the eternal ally or the perpetual enemies. Our interests are eternal and perpetual, and these interests it is our duty to follow."

Lord Palmerston (1848)

1. *The Traditional Policy.*

British Foreign Policy has enjoyed an ambivalent reputation for success and perfidy. In the past, numerous Americans abased themselves to the point of declaring that the honest American is always beaten by the British diplomat. Many Turks believe that the dictator, Kemal Ataturk, just before his death in 1938, enjoined his people to be as ready as possible for any future war, "and then, come what might, to stay on England's side, because that side was certain to win in the long run." [1] These tributes are often accompanied by a statement that British faithlessness and utter selfishness, qualities presumed to be unthinkable in Italians, Egyptians or Greeks, explain Britain's success. Selective indignation seizes upon the quotation from Palmerston, and, thereby, demonstrates the

---

[1] Lewis V. Thomas and Richard N. Frye, *The United States and Turkey and Iran* (Cambridge [Mass.], 1951), p. 89. A similar view is expressed in Ogden Nash's poem, "England Expects."

allegedly unique selfishness of Britain. This reputation has a venerable history, and it is, indeed, true that the objective of British foreign policy is to promote British interests. As these interests have been world-wide, it is easy for the Frenchman or the Pole to single out for denunciation a facet of British policy, at odds with his own country's interest. No single country's policy inevitably or frequently coincides with the general interest of all mankind. There is a tragic element in the rivalries of individuals and of nations.[2]

No mere nostalgia for the *Pax Britannica,* however, prompts the opinion that few nations have defined their interests with the moderation and flexibility of British policy. The British, for their part, have sometimes yielded to the temptation of believing that a policy for their world-wide interests was the proper policy for the world.

The self-regarding truth of Palmerston's remark is not the exclusive or predominant theme in statements on British policy. Palmerston himself frequently stressed British policy in terms of moral principles. But, as Britain's power has never been quantitatively sufficient for the protection of her many world-wide interests, British policy has very frequently been discussed in terms of Britain's capacity to support the policy. Even the Liberal leader, William Gladstone, who tended to moralize in politics, could on occasion balance resources of strength against the demands of commitments: "Why, gentlemen, there is not a country in the history of the world that has undertaken what we have undertaken . . . a small island at one extremity of the globe peoples the whole earth with its colonies. . . . We have undertaken to settle the affairs of about a fourth of

---

[2] Herbert Butterfield, "The Tragic Element in Modern International Conflict" in *History and Human Relations* (London, 1951), pp. 9-36.

the entire human race scattered over all the world." For this stupendous task there was available only the population of the United Kingdom, with a smaller population than Germany, the Austro-Hungarian Monarchy or Russia.[3]

The nature of British interests was well defined in Sir Eyre Crowe's Foreign Office memorandum of 1907: "The general character of England's foreign policy is determined by the immutable conditions of her geographical situation on the ocean flank of Europe as an island State with vast overseas colonies and dependencies, whose existence and survival as an independent community are inseparably bound up with the possession of preponderant sea power." The pervasive and formidable character of this power might very well draw the fears and jealousies of the world into a universal and hostile alliance. This danger can be averted only if the great naval power supports that first interest, common to all states, the preservation of their national independence. "It follows that England, more than any other non-insular Power, has a direct and positive interest in the maintenance of the independence of nations, and therefore must be the natural enemy of any country threatening the independence of others."

"Second only to the ideal of independence, nations have always cherished the right of free intercourse and trade in the world's markets, and in proportion as England champions the principle of the largest measure of general freedom of commerce, she undoubtedly strengthens her hold on the interested friendship of other nations, at least to the extent of making them feel less apprehensive of naval supremacy in the hands of a free trade England

---

[3] Gladstone's opening speech in the Midlothian campaign, Nov. 25, 1879, in J. H. Park, *British Prime Ministers of the Nineteenth Century* (New York, 1950), pp. 283-284.

than they would in the face of a predominately protectionist Power.

"History shows that the danger threatening the independence of this or that nation has generally arisen, at least in part, out of the momentary predominance of a neighboring State at once militarily powerful, economically efficient, and ambitious to extend its frontiers or spread its influence. . . . The only check on the abuse of political predominance derived from such a position has always consisted in the opposition of an equally formidable rival, or of a combination of several countries forming leagues of defence."[4]

Although this policy statement was widely regarded as immoral by the generation that produced the Munich Agreement, its liberal features are readily apparent. It is certainly not concerned with power for the sake of power, but with a balance of power for the security of an island whose trading interests favor peace and the independence of other states. The policy looks on Europe as an area to be balanced and checkmated. This policy requires great subtlety and understanding, for it may be difficult to distinguish growing strength from an aspiration to dominance. The upshot of perpetual balancing may be a free but broken, frustrated and defenseless Europe. Britain, in the past, has been a European bulwark against the subjugation of Europe by one power. Unfortunately, British policy was, therefore, almost inevitably opposed to European union. To implement this policy, Britain also looked on Europe as the area in which would be formed the Grand Alliance to destroy the disturber of the balance.

---

[4] "Memorandum of Sir Eyre Crowe," January 1, 1907, in *British Documents on the Origins of the War, 1914-1918,* edited by G. P. Gooch and Harold Temperley, Vol. III. (London, 1928), pp. 402-403.

Eyre Crowe's statement rightly associates the British Empire with "free intercourse and trade in the world markets." The British Empire and Commonwealth with its origins in mercantilist days, is, nonetheless, the creature of a freely trading world. The emphases upon commerce and sea power express the interests of an island kingdom, whose food and raw material imports were paid for not only by imperial trade but by income from the street car lines of Athens and Barcelona, Iranian banks, Argentine and Brazilian railways and the coastal shipping of China. Apart from coal the islanders had little to offer to the world market except the products of their skill and their capital savings.

2. *Changing Conditions and the Confusion of British Policy.*

The twentieth century saw the passing of Britain's industrial preeminence. Trade became more necessary than ever. But it encountered tariff barriers to trade and rivals of greater efficiency in Germany, Japan and the United States. Returns from investments overseas increasingly had to pay for the heavy excess of imports over exports. After 1935 the deficit was usually more than the invisible returns could match.[5]

The loss of industrial and commercial preeminence reduced the effectiveness of a balance of power policy. The development of the Japanese, German and American navies challenged that most necessary support of the policy, dominant seapower. But British interests remained the same, even in an age of neo-mercantilism. Her interest in world trade was to be pursued, albeit under more difficult conditions which eventually involved the abandonment of free trade and tariff preferences within the British Commonwealth.

---

[5] A. E. Kahn, *Great Britain in the World Economy* (New York, 1946), p. 126.

At the end of World War I Britain looked out on a greatly changed world. To the east, beyond defeated Germany and the ruins of the Austro-Hungarian and Ottoman Empires, was the continental mass of the Soviet Union, temporarily secluded from the major powers and the international conferences, but committed by doctrine and intrigue to challenging British world interests as Imperialism, the Dying Stage of Capitalism. This challenge was paralleled by a twofold imperial development; the restless nationalism of the colonial people and, after Britain's acquisition of former German and Turkish possessions as mandates held from the League of Nations, a defensive British attitude, which halted further imperial expansion and favored a gradual relaxing of the bonds and chains of empire. Britain favored the Open Door in East Asia. Hong-Kong and British investments in China were important interests to be maintained, not to be used as points for further advance. Singapore was the main British defense base; the China Seas and the Open Door were left to the protection of Japan and the United States. In Europe, prostrate Germany hindered the revival of world trade. British concern with German recovery and an instinctive and pedantic balance-of-power policy impelled Britain to work at cross-purposes with France. To the west was the continental United States soon to snarl world trade in its tariffs. The war had reduced Britain and Europe to debtors of the United States, a power not vitally and directly immersed in the world economy as Britain was.

The weakness of Britain was not immediately apparent. The United States continued to think of Britain as the world power, and American criticism of Britain was sometimes based on the assumption that, unlike the United States, Britain as a world power had a duty to act. While Germany was disarmed, Britain's power was considerable,

6

and Franco-British cooperation could have prevented the rearmament and strengthening of Germany. After 1936, however, the growing might of Germany overshadowed the peaceful and potential strength of Britain.

Changing industrial, financial and naval relations reduced the efficacy of the balance-of-power. Furthermore, between the wars British policy was diluted and confused by the existence of the League of Nations and the vogue of collective security. In 1924 the British Labour Government resolved to persuade the French to disarm by offering in the Geneva Protocol strong guarantees against aggression. These sanctions, in Labour's eyes, did not involve for Britain heavy military commitments, for Labour leaders had a misty, though powerful, belief in the efficacy of treaty deterrents. The Conservatives rejected this Geneva Protocol on the grounds that extensive collective security, which would include Central and Eastern Europe, was unrealistic and that the Protocol was too bellicose. It did, indeed, talk of war rather than of peace. Unfortunately, this searching criticism was not applied to the Locarno Agreements (1925), by which Germany, Belgium, Italy, France, and Britain guaranteed the adjoining frontiers of Germany, Belgium, and France, and the observance of the Versailles provisions about the Rhineland. These guarantees were meaningful in 1925 when Germany was disarmed, but this necessary precondition was not maintained. A not unfair judgment is that the Conservatives derided measures to implement collective security as unrealistic and, for a long time, too long, refused to disturb popular hopes in the League of Nations by initiating a large armament program.

The British National Government looked out on the totalitarian-ridden Europe of the mid-thirties with an apparent calmness that was unfortunately not based on a sober appraisal of German and Italian realities. In response to public opinion the British government in 1935 supported the League of Nations' economic sanctions against Fascist Italy, which had attacked Ethiopia. But the effort was made half-heartedly and in fear of being committed to an Italian war which would leave Germany and Japan free to expand. Failure disclosed that sanctions, which Anthony Eden had described as a "bloodless device to bring aggressors to reason,"[6] were "mid-summer madness" and doomed the League.

Foreign policy became an issue in British domestic politics. Although there were many currents of thought in the Labour Party, it believed, broadly speaking, in collective security.[7] Because the National Government did not support collective security, the Labour Party refused to vote for the Government's armament program. This attitude involved considerable irony, for the Labour Party was very ready to demand that the Government take a strong stand on many issues.

The Government's position was well expressed by Viscount Halifax. "Unless you are prepared on the one hand to say, 'I will fight in every case on behalf of peace, which is one and indivisible,' or on the other hand to say, ' I will only fight when I am myself the victim of attack'—unless you are prepared to take one of those two positions there

---

[6] *Parliamentary Debates,* House of Commons, Vol. 311, May 6, 1936, clmn. 1736.

[7] Clement Attlee argued that the Locarno Agreements evaded collective security, and, in seeking to limit Britain's commitments, embarked upon alliances and power politics. "The country is more interested in the frontiers of Holland and Belgium, because of the historic position, than in the frontiers of Czechoslovakia or the frontiers of Poland. The League position is that we are out to defend the rule of law and not particular territories." *Parliamentary Debates,* House of Commons, Vol. 310, March 26, 1936, clmn. 1534.

[8] *Parliamentary Debates,* House of Lords, Vol. 104, March 3, 1937, clmn. 498.

is an inevitable no-man's land of uncertainty lying between which is quite incapable, as I think, of antecedent definition."[8]

3. Munich and Its Consequences.

Neville Chamberlain, who in 1937 became Prime Minister, was prepared to support rearmament, but not on a scale to match Germany's. He believed that Britain was still in the painful process of economic recovery, that if Britain was "to follow Winston's advice and sacrifice our commerce to the manufacture of arms, we should inflict a certain injury on our trade from which it would take generations to recover."[9] Mr. Chamberlain, who increasingly acted as his own Foreign Secretary, could not yet bring himself to face the fact that in Bagehot's phrase this was "not the age for arithmetic."

Mr. Chamberlain regarded the armaments program as a costly and distasteful necessity. It was an earnest of Britain's determination to be considered in European affairs. It would support his effort to restore European confidence in the manner of Locarno. He was prepared to recognize the "legitimate interests" of Germany, on condition that the necessary changes be made peacefully.[10] Even after the Nazi career of conquest began in Austria, the British Prime Minister remained calm. When Czechoslovakia became the next objective of Hitler's ambition, Mr. Chamberlain pressed the Czechs to make concessions to the Germans. Not balance of power, but appeasement and the restoration of confidence

---

[9] Keith Feiling, *The Life of Neville Chamberlain* (London, 1946), p. 314.

[10] "It is the predominant British view that any aim which Germany may legitimately set herself beyond her Eastern borders can be accomplished by peaceful means, and could only risk defeat in a general upheaval if attempted by any other means." *The Times,* Feb. 17, 1938.

were the objectives of British policy. The remote possibility of a politically divided and embittered France, standing by her ally, Czechoslovakia, was provided for by firmly reminding the timid French Premier Daladier of France's feeble will for battle.[11]

The result of this policy was the Munich settlement, which the British diplomatic historian, Sir Charles Webster, has called "the greatest deviation from British policy that has occurred in the last 150 years."[12] The Munich agreement marked a startling reversal of power and prestige in Europe. The crisis took shape because of Hitler's readiness for war and Mr. Chamberlain's determination that change should be made peacefully. British policy, in the words of John Buchan, quoted approvingly by the British Foreign Minister, Lord Halifax, involved "perpetually telling Benes what we might *not* do in the event of trouble; and of tactfully reminding the Germans of what we *might* do."[13] British policy had reached the fatuous dilemma posed by Britain's Ambassador to Germany, Sir Nevile Henderson: "If we decline to admit self-determination we must face world war; if we recognize it, we must coerce Czechoslovakia or sit by and watch her coerced by Germany." It was only on "method and procedure" that "we can hope to extract 'concessions' from Germany."[14]

---

[11] The Prime Minister wrote in his diary on March 20, 1938: "With a French Government in which one can not have the slightest confidence and which I suspect to be in closest touch with our Opposition, with the Russians stealthily and cunningly pulling all the strings behind the scenes to get us involved in war with Germany." Keith Feiling, *op. cit.*, p. 347.

[12] *United Kingdom Policy* (London, 1950), p. 11; see M. A. Fitzsimons, "The Masque of Uncertainty: Britain and Munich," *The Review of Politics*, XII (1950), 489-505.

[13] *Documents on British Foreign Policy, 1919-1939*, edited by E. L. Woodward and Rohan Butler, Third Series, II (London, 1949), no. 587, pp. 54-56.

[14] *Ibid.*, no. 917, p. 367.

The dilemma was fatuous because the security of Britain and Europe and not self-determination was the issue. Eyre Crowe was belied in his assumption that Britain with the regularity "of a law of nature" would always throw her weight on the side opposed to any state aspiring to political dictatorship in Europe. Czechoslovakia was dismembered, her military strength was disrupted and, eventually, her munitions plants served the Nazi war machine.[15]

The subsequent rupture of the Munich agreement in March, 1939, when Hitler took over the remnants of the Czech state, caused Mr. Chamberlain to enter into a profusion of commitments to Poland, Greece, and Rumania, among others. The guarantee to Poland actually gave the initiative for choosing peace or war to the Polish Government. Later, logical efforts to secure Soviet assistance foundered, when the Soviet Union secretly agreed with Nazi Germany on the partition of Poland. By September 3, 1939, Britain and France were at war with Germany.

Winston Churchill, who very early had exposed the consequence of British policy as the weakening of France, bitterly attacked the appeasement program.[16] It had made the enemy more implacable and stronger, and war on disadvantageous terms more likely. "Here was the righteous cause deliberately and with a refinement of inverted artistry committed to mortal battle after its assets and advantages had been so improvidently squandered. . . . There may even be a worse case. You may have to fight when there is no hope of victory, because it is better to perish than live as slaves."[17]

---

[15] The published British Foreign Office Documents do not reveal any calculations that Germany would soon be involved in war with Russia.

[16] See his speech of March 14, 1934, in *Parliamentary Debates,* House of Commons, Vol. 287, especially clmn. 397.

[17] *The Gathering Storm* (Boston, 1948), pp. 347-348.

4. *The Ordeal of War and the Design of Peace.*

Even war itself did not end the miscalculations of Mr. Chamberlain's Government, which expected a long war of strangulation of Germany and a final Anglo-French push against the German homeland. After the fall of France had belied these hopes, the new Prime Minister Churchill, on whom had fallen the responsibility for rescuing Britain from the consequences of policies which he had opposed, made this pledge: "Czechs, Poles, Norwegians, Dutch, Belgians, have joined their cause to our own. All these shall be restored."[18] London became the seat of a multitude of free governments, whose numbers swelled as Hitler swept over Europe. These promises of restoration were, at best, only brave aspirations until Russia and the United States were drawn into the war.

Churchill's defiance of the Nazi tyrant was sustained by his hope of American support and intervention. But the defiance was costly and eventual victory was paid for in a grievous weakening of British economy and power.[19] In the eighteen months before Lend-Lease, Britain liquidated much of her foreign investments in order to maintain the British war effort. There began that complicated phase of British financial problems called the sterling balances, as Britain assumed control of the hard currencies earned by countries tied to sterling. In the course of the war, therefore, Britain's creditor relationship with such countries as Egypt and India was reversed.

The Nazi attack on the Soviet Union (June 22, 1941)

---

[18] Speech of June 18, 1940, to the House of Commons, quoted in W. S. Churchill, *The Gathering Storm* (Boston, 1949), p. 225.

[19] The details of British-American relations in 1939-1940 are described in William L. Langer and S. Everett Gleason, *The Challenge to Isolationism, 1937-1940* (New York, 1952).

marked the beginnings of the Grand Alliance which Churchill had urged in the years before the war. This alliance was a wholly reluctant wedding on the battlefield. Soviet demands ran counter to the policies of the United States, the power with which Churchill sought close association. When, at the end of 1941, Foreign Minister Anthony Eden went to Moscow, Britain was asked to recognize a large number of territorial changes. To have done so would have conflicted with the British-American statement of Peace Aims made in the Atlantic Charter (August, 1941). Eden refused to give British approval to Soviet expansionism. Later, when it appeared that a new German drive would be launched against "the only country that is heavily engaged with the German armies," Churchill changed his mind. "Under the pressure of events, I did not feel that this moral position could be physically maintained."[20] Nonetheless, firm American opposition forestalled this concession, and no territorial provisions were in the Anglo-Soviet Treaty signed on May 26, 1942. The treaty provided for an alliance of twenty years and an agreement to work together for peace and prosperity in Europe.

Territorial changes were not mentioned because American policy was opposed to territorial and political settlements during the war, and American policy prevailed because the United States had finally entered the war. This development made possible the Declaration of the United Nations (Jan. 1, 1942) by which the Soviet Union, also, affirmed adherence to the Atlantic Charter.

The United Nations was a wartime coalition, pledged to the disarmament of the aggressors, "pending the establishment of a wider and permanent system of general security." The details and outlines of that system were to be arranged

---

[20]   Churchill, *The Hinge of Fate* (Boston, 1950), p. 327.

later. At first, Churchill's long-held views about a world organization based on regional blocs portended an agreement with the United States, for Roosevelt and Sumner Welles held similar views.[21]

Churchill's views of the postwar world took account of the continuation of power politics. At Washington he had said: "It was important to recreate a strong France, for the prospects of having no strong country on the map between England and Russia was not attractive."[22] His remark that Coudenhove-Kalergi's ideas on European union "had much to recommend them" was significant. That author's *Pan-Europa* (1923) had argued that Europe faced "the following alternative: either to overcome all national hostilities and consolidate in a federal union, or sooner or later to succumb to a Russian conquest." Churchill, of course, did not favor federal union but "a coalition resistance to any act of aggression . . . no one can predict with certainty that the victors will never quarrel among themselves." His sober hope for Big Three Unity was that comradeship in suffering and the hideous prospect of another war would cause the leading powers to make "the most intense effort . . . to prolong their honourable association."[23]

Within this Big Three dominance there was to be the imbalance necessary to the balance of power policy. Britain and the United States would be bound in that fraternal association which, to Churchill, represented the fundamental

[21] Sumner Welles, *Seven Decisions That Shaped History* (New York, 1950), pp. 184-185. Before 1943 Roosevelt largely had thought in terms of an Anglo-American policing of the world. With grave doubts Churchill agreed to Roosevelt's later insistence that China be numbered among the great powers who were to decide "all the basic decisions affecting the maintenance of world order." *Ibid.*, p. 188.

[22] Conversation with American offiicals and Senators, May 22, 1943; *The Hinge of Fate* (Boston, 1950), p. 803.

[23] Churchill's notes, "Morning Thoughts," *The Hinge of Fate*, pp. 711-712.

assumption of postwar British policy. The fostering of that association involved a perplexing interplay of American and British policies concerning a world organization, the Mediterranean, and Asia.

Roosevelt, though initially favorable to regional blocs, came to favor an international organization, open eventually to all the states of the world. This view prevailed and reenforced United States' opposition to making political and territorial decisions before the War's end. In February, 1943, Churchill sent Roosevelt his "Morning Thoughts: Note on Post-War Security" which presented a case for a world organization based on the dominance of the Big Three associated with representatives of regional blocs. He favored a strong France as the continental basis of this new Grand Alliance. In the second half of March, 1943, Churchill publicly proposed the same arrangement, inevitably in less specific terms. In Washington during May, 1943, Churchill repeated his proposal and indicated his hope that the United States would also be represented on the European Council.

The American policy of delaying political decisions and settlements until the War's end risked a great danger. Even with the best will in the world, the very progress of armies forced some political decisions. Military occupation meant an inevitable control which certainly had political aspects. With this in mind the British government in July, 1943, favored the creation of a European Commission "to coordinate the execution of surrender or armistice terms" and to deal with arrangements for European security, and economic integration.[24] Hull opposed this, for he was against political

---

[24] Hull, *The Memoirs of Cordell Hull* (New York, 1948), II, 1640-1642. The Australian war correspondent, Chester Wilmot in *The Struggle For Europe* (New York, 1952), blames American naivete for the weakened Allied position after the war.

15

wartime decisions and in favor of a universal organization. Hull's views prevailed over Roosevelt's earlier opinion,[25] and there followed the Moscow Declaration in favor of an international organization.

There was no sharply defined conflict in all this, for the regional organization was compatible with the universal organization. Moreover, during the war, the British Government could not be precise about a European bloc. The concentration of European governments-in-exile in London promoted considerable discussion of European union, which Churchill favored. In 1944 Anthony Eden pointed out the difficulties of promoting European Union during wartime: "We have had certain informal discussions about our future relations, and these will be pursued in due course. . . . These Governments have all to return to their own countries; they have to seek fresh authority; perhaps re-form, perhaps change, their personnel; so deliberately we did not carry the conversations beyond the general point that we, for our part, are ready to enter into close association with them, as they are with us, to guarantee the future peace of Europe and to play our part in dealing with our common problems."[26]

The interplay of American and British interests in the Mediterranean produced sharper conflicts. The United States was associated with the Middle East Supply Center, which was established in April, 1941, to assure the distribution of essential goods among the Middle Eastern states, and to regulate available shipping and port space in the interests of the United Nations' miltary effort and of the civilian needs of the region. In this activity some Americans and

---

[25] "The more advanced regional ideas of President Roosevelt and Prime Minister Churchill, however, might lead to questions of balance of power." *Ibid.*, II, 1646.

[26] *Parliamentary Debates,* House of Commons, Nov. 29, 1944, clmn.

many Frenchmen believed that they saw a plot to extend British influence and to tie the area more closely to the pound sterling.[27]

British and Russian troops occupied Iran, and were soon joined by American technical troops for supervision of supplies to Russia. All parties were pledged to the independence of Iran.

To American leaders Britain's concern with the security of Mediterranean communications sometimes appeared as the fostering of British imperial interests at the expense of a direct blow at the German Army in France. Churchill feared the revival of political life in Italy and was opposed to American proposals calling for the rapid broadening of the Badoglio government.[28] In the face of American misgivings, he made a spheres-of-influence agreement whereby Russia recognized Greece as wholly in the British sphere (Oct. 1944). This arrangement had been prepared earlier, when the Royalist (and British) cause in Greece had been weakened by a mutiny of the Greek armed forces in Egypt and by discord between the Royalists-in-exile and the leftist resistance forces in Greece. After British forces had liberated

[27] For the clash of Anglo-American interests in the Middle East, see the valuable article by Martin W. Wilmington, "The Middle East Supply Center: A Reappraisal," *The Middle East Journal*, VI (1952), 144-166. The bitter experience of the French is recorded in Général Catroux, *Dans la bataille de Méditerranée* (Paris, 1949). In a tedious book, Mary Borden, the novelist wife of General Spears, British wartime minister to Syria and Lebanon, has reflected British suspicions of the French. *Journey Down a Blind Alley* (New York, 1946.)

[28] Churchill to Roosevelt, Feb. 13, 1944: "This Italian Government will obey our directions far more than any other that we may laboriously constitute. On the other hand, it has more power over the Fleet, Army officials, etc., than anything else which can be set up out of the worn-out debris of political parties, none of whom have the slightest title by election or prescription. A new Italian Government will have to make its reputation with the Italian people by standing up to us." Churchill, *Closing the Ring* (Boston, 1951), pp. 497-498.

parts of Greece, the returning Greek government in December, 1944, was challenged by an uprising, which was suppressed. Greece was saved from Communist domination at the cost of passing under Rightist and Royalist control while the United States remained a disapproving spectator.[29] Roosevelt, Hull and Stettinius expressed their distaste for British "power politics."[30] Elsewhere, Yugoslavia was lost to Tito and the Balkans passed into the hands of the Red Army. Whether the agreement with Russia was necessary for the rescue of Greece is debatable. British wisdom was also tempered by limited power. On Feb. 27, 1945, Churchill told the House of Commons; "While the war is on, we give help to anyone who can kill a Hun; when the war is over we look to the solution of a free, unfettered democratic election."[31]

In the Far East Britain's weakness was glaringly apparent. Pearl Harbor solved the question of the United States' entry into the war, but Britain was swept from all of South-

---

[29] This account has simplified the tropical lushness of Greek complexites. The British Ambassador to Greece, Sir Reginald Leeper, has given the official apologia in *When Greek Meets Greek* (London, 1950). The chief of the British Military Mission to Occupied Greece, Colonel C. M. Woodhouse, presents a more plausible and critical account in *Apple of Discord* (London, 1950). Field Marshal Wilson's *Eight Years Overseas, 1939-1947* (London, 1949) considers political matters only as they affect the armed struggle against the Axis. A strong criticism of British policy appears in L. S. Stavrianos, *Greece: American Dilemma and Opportunity* (Chicago, 1952). He does justice to the tangle of Greek factions, but, I believe, underestimates the Communist character of ELAS. Perhaps the fairest statement is that British policy engendered Communist strength, which was, then, weakened by forceful British action. The account in Hugh Seton-Watson, *The East European Revolution* (London, 1950) is judicious.

[30] Elliott Roosevelt, *As He Saw It* (New York, 1946); Hull, *The Memoirs of Cordell Hull*, II, 1451-1459; E. R. Stettinius, *Roosevelt & the Russians* (Garden City, 1949), pp. 10-13; Sherwood, *Roosevelt and Hopkins* (New York, 1948), pp. 837, 839, 843. Winston Churchill defended his policy in "If I Were an American," *Life* (April 14, 1947).

[31] *Parliamentary Debates*, House of Commons, Vol. 408, Feb. 27, 1945, clmn. 1281.

east Asia, Burma, and Malaya. Some Burmese and Indians welcomed Japan as a liberator from the European imperialists. Japan's initial victory was a fillip to Asian nationalism. The vocal political element in India was not associated with the fight against the Axis, even though British Indian armies continued to fight.

Britain, then, apart from some guerilla fighters in Malaya, was out of most of the Far East and Southeast Asia.[32] This revelation of British weakness caused Australia to press for the creation of a Pacific War Council in Washington. At first, the British Government would only agree to set up a Pacific Council in London as an advisory group to the Combined Chiefs of Staff in Washington. "The only plausible explanation appears to be London's extreme reluctance to transfer control of Pacific strategy to American hands."[33] But the fall of Singapore reconciled the British to overall American control of the war in the Pacific and MacArthur became supreme commander of the United Nations' forces in the Southwest Pacific. Anzac and British forces participated in the fighting in New Guinea and Burma, but the major fight against Japan was an American show, in which, oddly enough, the British were barely welcome.

The enormous strains of a global war, meshed in a multitude of local conflicts, were eased in the hopeful facade of

----

[32] Churchill's war decisions in this area have been bitterly criticized by David H. James, a British intelligence officer: "It appears that we were ready to rely on a few head-hunters, a few squads of volunteers without rifles, and three companies of infantry. . . . Blow-pipes, parangs, and fixed bayonets would be sufficient—on the assumption that the Japanese would land with nothing more than bow and arrow, and samurai sword, and assault the beaches in sampans from a fleet of junks." *The Rise and Fall of the Japanese Empire* (London, 1951), pp. 195, 198-201. An even more severe criticism is made by Captain Russell Grenfell in *Main Fleet To Singapore* (New York, 1952), Chapters VI-X.

[33] Werner Levi, *American-Australian Relations* (Minneapolis, 1947), p. 152.

Big Three Unity and Cooperation. This bracing concept of wartime was the foundation stone of the proposals for world organization at Teheran. There Roosevelt explained his views about the three policemen. When the subject of international organization came up, the United States proposed that parties to a dispute should not be allowed to vote. This was essential to a system of collective security. The compromise arrangement at Yalta, whereby a permanent member of the Security Council could not vote in the discussion of peaceful solutions of a dispute, but could veto any enforcement measures, made the dream of collective security more dream-like. Big Three Unity became all the more imperative.

The advance of the Russian armies in 1945 worried Churchill. Poland fell to the Soviet sphere and Eastern Europe was apparently doomed to the same fate. Churchill's cables to Washington after the victory in the West aroused the fear that he might act hastily and endanger the unity of the Big Three. The former American Ambassador to the Soviet Union, Joseph Davies, was sent to get Churchill's views in preparation for the forthcoming Big Three conferences. Churchill was "genuinely fearful of what would happen if American troops were withdrawn from Europe," leaving the continent "prostrate and at the mercy of the Red Army and of Communism." Davies had replied that Churchill's fears were tantamount to an admission that Hitler was right.[34] Indeed, Churchill's forebodings were evident in a broadcast speech (May 13, 1945), in which he spoke little of Russia and much of American cooperation and power; he feared the possible distortion of democratic ideals and re-

---

[34] Joseph Davies' account of Churchill's views in May, 1945, as reported from the notes of Admiral Leahy in *I Was There* (New York, 1950), pp. 369-370, 378-379.

ferred to the islanders' opportunity of standing out alone against continental tyrants.[35]

On the Continent France had been liberated. Franco-British relations, the cornerstone of Western Union, were strained. Britain favored French participation in the occupation of Germany, but different approaches to the problems of the Middle East caused a bitter controversy. Britain in sponsoring the Arab League, a xenophobic and anti-Zionist coalition, hoped to maintain a directing influence in the Middle East. To the French the Arab League appeared to menace their own position in the Levant and North Africa. The showdown came when French forces bombarded Damascus. In return for French recognition of Syrian independence, France had sought military and naval concessions from Syria. The bombardment occurred after riots had followed the arrival of French reinforcements. On May 31, 1945, British armed forces intervened. In placating the Arab world and the Syrians, Britain confirmed French mistrust. De Gaulle described Britain's objective as an attempt "to polarize on France the hostile movements of opinion in the Near East." Churchill curtly justified his action: "I also explained [to De Gaulle] that we had recognized France's special position in the Levant, but that does not mean we have undertaken to enforce that special position."[36]

At the moment the talk of European union seemed hollow. But Churchill's interest in a strong France had implications for Germany. Neither the strength of France nor that of Britain could be solidly based on the destruction of the German economy. Churchill objected that the Morgenthau Plan meant "England's being chained to a dead

---

[35] Churchill, *Victory* (Boston, 1946), pp. 171-179; for Admiral Leahy's misrepresentation of this talk, see *I Was There*, p. 381.
[36] *New York Times*, June 6 and 20, 1945.

body."[37] The British Prime Minister, perhaps bewildered by Roosevelt's approval of the Plan, and obsessed by Britain's impoverishment, may have been moved by the promise of American aid. At any rate he did agree to the Morgenthau Plan.[38] Another consideration in this action was the prospect of removing the competition of German industry. But even at Yalta, Churchill had been cautious about German reparations, and had opposed acceptance of the Soviet figure of $20,000,000,000 as a basis for discussion.[39]

When the British occupied Germany, their more just and realistic approach was confused by the contradictory policies of the United States. It is certain that the British Government envisaged a long occupation and provided a very large staff for the occupation work. When the occupation took place, the British were shocked by the destruction which had been wrought. Confronted by an appaling disintegration they grimly set themselves to the inescapable work of economic revival, the very development which Morgenthau had feared.

At the Potsdam Conference, the wartime front of Big Three unity was maintained for the last time.[40] In London shortly before the Conference, one of the saddest scenes of the war was acted out. As portent of past failures and future bitterness, the London offices of the Polish Govern-

---

[37]   Hull, *The Memoirs of Cordell Hull*, II, pp. 1610, 1614-1615, 1622; Henry L. Stimson and McGeorge Bundy, *On Active Service in Peace and War* (New York, 1948), pp. 568-570, 577-578.

[38]   Fred Smith, "The Rise & Fall of the Morgenthau Plan," *United Nations World*, I (March, 1947), 32-37. This article is not wholly reliable, but its account of Churchill's comments is plausible.

[39]   Stettinius, *op. cit.*, pp. 255, 263-266.

[40]   The works by James F. Byrnes and Admiral Leahy recall the high hopes of cooperation prevailing at the time. John R. Deane, *The Strange Alliance* (New York, 1947), p. 267, notes that at Potsdam the American military men were particularly confident of wholehearted cooperation.

ment in Exile were closed, for the British Government had recognized another Polish Government, more acceptable to the Soviet Union.

5. *The Promise of the Labour Victory.*

Meanwhile, the leaders and party in control of the British Government had changed. In the elections of July, 1945, the Labour Party won a substantial majority. As a result, Britain faced the problems of reconstruction with a government that emphasized security and welfare. The remarkable absence of change in foreign policy may be seen in the presence of the Labour leader, Clement Attlee, during the whole of the Potsdam Conference. At first, he was present as leader of His Majesty's Loyal Opposition, and, after the announcement of the election results, as Prime Minister. In the wartime coalition government Attlee had been Deputy Prime Minister. Thus, the leaders of the Labour Party had been committed to the major foreign policy decisions of Churchill's coalition government. Labour's Foreign Secretary, Ernest Bevin, shared Eden's opposition to the Russian *fait accompli* in transferring parts of East Germany to Poland.[41]

To many, the Labour victory appeared to seal the promises of continued accord with Russia, for, as the election slogan went, left understands left. British leftists had a momentary vision of a Europe regenerated from Fascism, capitalism, and power politics, for socialist theory attributed the world's ills, including power politics and war, to self-seek-

---

[41] For a characteristic example of wishful reporting see the *New Statesman and Nation*, August 11, 1945, where it is stated that Bevin's appearance at Potsdam appreciably improved the Anglo-Soviet atmosphere. Actually, Bevin's manner was so aggressive that Truman and Byrnes wondered how they would get along with the Foreign Secretary. Byrnes, *Speaking Frankly* (New York, 1947), p. 79.

ing capitalism. The British Labour Party, unlike the Communist parties of the world, has few devoted students of power. The Labour leaders have emphasized their democratic character and the constitutional gradualness of their socialism.[42]

Presumably, a Socialist Government would not be moved by considerations of power and international strategy. Leftist thinking held that the foreign policy of the Labour Government would be something new in the world, and above all, that it would depart from "the continuity of British Foreign Policy."[43] Labour's foreign policy would be unaggressive and dedicated to collective security. In August, 1945, these hopes were trumpeted aloud by Harold Laski during a visit to France. Such widely held views did influence the character of Bevin's policy statements, but not the eventual formation of policy.[44]

---

[42] See E. A. Shils, "Britain and the World," *Review of Politics,* VII (1945), 505-524, and M. A. Fitzsimons, "British Labour in Search of a Socialist Foreign Policy," *Review of Politics,* XII (1950), 197-214. Professor Sam Davis of Washington University (St. Louis) will soon publish an excellent study of Labour's thinking on foreign policy in the nineteen-thirties.

[43] Professor Harold Laski, a member of Labour's National Executive, said during the election campaign: "I want to emphasize that the Labour Party is at no point committed to the doctrine of continuity in foreign policy." In another speech he repeated: "We do not propose to accept the Tory doctrine of the continuity of foreign policy, because we have no interest in the continuity of Conservative policy." *The Times,* July 3, 1945. Laski's and the left's sense of guiltlessness about the past is in sharp contrast with the following remark of Bevin, made in the Commons in 1941: "I have said on the platform a dozen times that if anyone asks me who is responsible for the mess in which we find ourselves in this country, I say 'All of us.' I say that, because we all refused to face the facts, and landed ourselves in it; because we were hoping against hope, that this trouble would not arise. It did arise, and it is just as well to acknowledge it, and having acknowledged it, to do our damnedest to get out of it." Quoted by Jack Cherry in *All the Cards on the Table* (London, no date), p. 26.

[44] In 1937 when Labour was in opposition, Clement Attlee had rejected continuity. *The Labour Party in Perspective* (London, 1937), pp. 226-227. The foreign policy statements of the Labour Party and the foreign policy of

This belief in a departure from "the continuity of British Foreign Policy" was the impractical product of naively benevolent thinking.[45] Attlee and Bevin had been members of the Coalition Government and shared responsibility for foreign policy decisions. Bevin's acceptance of continuity, of Churchillian and Conservative policy, was made manifest during the first parliamentary debate on foreign policy when he assented to Anthony Eden's statement that in the Coalition Cabinet Bevin and he had never differed on any important issue of foreign policy.[46]

---

the Labour Government are not at all the same thing. The Labour Party's programs are formulated by the Party's National Executive and, as a rule, approved by the Party Conference. Prior to 1945, these programs, for example on Palestine, reflect the fact that Labour was an opposition party. The foreign policy of the Labour Government was formulated by Bevin in consultation with the Foreign Office staff and by the Cabinet. This policy, in turn, required the support of the Parliamentary Labour Party, which could express its dissatisfaction and press for modifications but could not openly oppose Bevin's policy without overturning the Labour Government and jeopardizing Labour's domestic program as well.

[45] Leonard Woolf, a veteran writer on Socialist problems and policies, criticized the Labour Party's statement, "The International Postwar Settlement," as a mixed ambiguous thing. "The result is that the policy is confused and inconsistent, speaking with two contradictory voices, one that of international socialism, and the other of an apologetic socialism which assures the world that it is just as realist and strong as Tory Nationalism and not really very different from it." He insisted that Labour's foreign policy "must be founded uncompromisingly on Socialist principles." Woolf, "The International Post War Settlement," Fabian Publications, Research Series, No. 85 (London, 1944), p. 3. But Woolf gives no outline of what a Socialist foreign policy would be. He suggests that it would be unaggressive and benevolent, except in the face of aggressive capitalism. But should benevolence be transformed into surrender, if benevolence is met by suspicious self-seeking? The leftists saw Britain's role as the leader of a Socialist Europe. If Britain should prop up her dying capitalism by allying with the United States, her socialism would be thwarted. "The struggle against British capitalism and against the suppression of the European revolution is also a struggle against Yankee Imperialism." John Strawhorn, "We Can Make Britain Socialist," *Left* (March, 1945), 354. The extreme, non-Communist left did not wish to think in terms of real power.

[46] *Parliamentary Debates*, Vol. 413, House of Commons, Aug. 20, 1945, clmn. 312.

Bevin's difficulties in handling foreign policy came from his own Party. In defending the action of British troops against the Greek Communists, Bevin attacked the sentimental radicalism of his colleagues. If Labour won the next election, it would learn that "you cannot govern the world by emotionalism."[47] Shortly before the elections, Bevin and Attlee attempted to sober the Party Conference at Blackpool by emphasizing the magnitude and bewildering variety of Britain's problems. To his Party colleagues Bevin, in characteristic prose, sounded a note that was to reappear constantly in his later policy statements. "You will have to form a government, which is at the centre of a great Empire and commonwealth of Nations, which touches all parts of the world, and which will have to deal, through the diplomatic, commercial and labour machinery with every race and with every difficulty, and everyone of them has a different outlook upon life. . . . I would ask the Conference to bear this in mind. Revolutions do not change geography, and revolutions do not change geographical needs." He favored a Peace Conference, and proposed to his Russian friends: "Round the table we must get, but do not present us with *faits accomplis* when we get there." "In our Foreign Policy we stand, as Attlee has said, for collective security. Collective security involves commitments, and I do beg Labour not to bury its head in the sand."[48]

Bevin took pride in his practical sense, and occasionally suggested that ideology might explain why some foreigners acted strangely or outrageously. He was aware of the com-

---

[47] *New York Times,* Dec. 14, 1944.

[48] Fearing the consequences of Labour's previous anti-imperialism, Bevin added: "I would, however, say to our Indian friends that "if we do get a Labour Government, do not put more pressure on us than you did upon the other Parties." *Report of the 44th Annual Conference of the Labour Party* (London, 1945), pp. 107-108, 115-118.

petitive character of the modern state system, and while he was prepared to cooperate with the states of the world, he recognized that until a genuine system of collective security prevailed, it would be suicidal to fail to maintain British interests. He brought to foreign policy the realism which he had previously displayed in building up the vast Transport Workers Union. He considered problems in terms of the welfare of British workingmen. Their welfare, as he saw it, was dependent on the preservation of British interests throughout the world. Against charges of imperialism he justified his defense of Britain's position in the Middle East by relating that position to the wages[49] of British workers.

His mind reposed in massive certainties, supported by a powerful self-righteousness. His train of thought, as he explained it, was sometimes exasperatingly obscure.[50]

The permanent officials of the British Foreign Office found their new chief to be a workingman who was always

---

[49] Speaking to a Labour Conference, Bevin said: "Reference was made by one speaker in connection with the Middle East to the fact that we ought to hand this over to an international concern. I am not going to be a party to voluntarily putting all British interests in a pool and everybody else sticking to his own. The standard of life and the wages of the workmen of this country are dependent upon these things, as indeed they are upon other things." *Report of the 46th Annual Conference of the Labour Party* (London, 1947), p. 176.

[50] An interesting evaluation appeared in *The Round Table*, No. 165 (December, 1951), 18-19; "he had the liberal habit of protesting grandiloquently on occasions on which action was impossible, and he often showed very little finesse in carrying out policies which he had decided were right. He thought in large and at times unduly clear terms, and dealt in phrases like "resistance to aggression" which neither improve the atmosphere of diplomacy nor throw any light on its problems. Although he was always ready to negotiate with Russia he left the impression of lacking the suppleness and realism which would have made negotiations fruitful. . . . He met uncompromising logic with uncompromising logic, and by so doing squandered one of the most formidable weapons of British diplomacy, the national talent for confusing issues. But all this is as nothing compared with his skill in carrying the Labour party behind a policy which, though it now seems obviously right, was hostile to that party's tradition."

ready to assert Britain's interests. His subsequent popularity with the Conservatives was their tribute to his defense of British interests, although their support sometimes embarrassed Mr. Bevin's relations with his own Party. Bevin's resistance to Soviet policies could not readily be ascribed to capitalist Conservatism's hostility to the Communist Fatherland. A trade unionist background provided some assurances that Anglo-Soviet difficulties involved the general interests of Britain rather than narrow capitalist interests. This was "the importance of being Ernest."

In the immediate tasks of foreign affairs Bevin was prepared to advocate collective security and to maintain British positions. For the moment, there could be little thought of balance. There was no material for a Grand Alliance on the continent. Nor could the weight of Britain be decisive on the scales. Britain's war for survival was won at great cost. Apart from the vast work of domestic reconstruction and the replacement of wornout or obsolete plants Britain's credit relationship to the world had disastrously changed. More than $\frac{1}{4}$ of her overseas investment had been liquidated. External debts, including sterling balances, amounted to £2,879,000,000. British shipping resources had been reduced by 30%.[51] The British economy was no longer to be strongly supported by earnings and returns from abroad, and at the same time the debtor British economy was ill-equipped for the necessary effort to increase production and exports.[52]

Britain in winning the War, also lost its status as a great power. After the War the United States was apparently richer than ever. During the War its national production

---

[51] W. K. Hancock and M. M. Gowing, *British War Economy* (London, 1949), p. 548.
[52] Howard S. Ellis, *The Economics of Freedom* (New York, 1950), p. 91.

28

had increased by an amount that may have equalled total British production. The power of the Soviet Union was not so immediately apparent, but as Churchill neatly put it: "After this war the armed might of Russia has emerged steadily year by year, almost month by month, as a rock shows more and more above an ebbing tide."[53] Britain was now a power with world interests, not a world power. The great powers were two continental masses, inaccessible to the power of any coalition of lesser states that could be raised against them.

---

[53] Speech of November 30, 1950, in Hans Morgenthau, *In Defense of the National Interest* (New York), p. 278.

CHAPTER TWO

The Troubled Twilight of Big Three Unity

"Soon everyone will be civilized."
"Why so, Lord Johnson?"
"Of course, they must be — they like to be." Johnson says.
"You will see how they like it. All men like to be civilized."
Joyce Cary, *Mister Johnson* (Harper, 1951), p. 89.

1. *The Frustrated Peace and the Cold War.*

A few weeks after the final victory of the peace-loving nations over the Axis aggressors, the Council of Foreign Ministers met (Sept. 11-Oct. 2, 1945) in London to begin the drafting of peace treaties. The first euphoria of victory was receding, when the Conference broke up in an utter stalemate. The very first venture towards establishing peace was frustrated. The British knew better than most people that victory marks the end of coalitions and alliances. But the last months of the war and the first months of peace progressively revealed Soviet hostility and not a mere lessening of cordiality. The scattered interests of Britain felt the first impact of the Cold War.

Bevin had been under no illusion about the unity of the Big Three. But the sustained Soviet diplomatic and propaganda offensive against British interests portended difficult times for a weakened Britain. If the overture was so grim, would the post-war drama be a tragedy?

At Potsdam the representatives of the Soviet Union had expressed a disturbing interest in the Mediterranean.[1] As it was developed, this concern centered around four points: the Dodecanese Islands and the Italian Colonies, control of the Turkish Straits and objections to British troops in Greece. This unwelcome concern for the Mediterranean was paralleled by a vigorous bid to expand Russian influence in northern Iran, where in 1944 Soviet agents had unsuccessfully sought to get oil concessions. At Potsdam, the British had supported an early withdrawal of forces from Iran. The Soviet Union agreed to an immediate withdrawal from Teheran, and to discuss the stages of full withdrawal at the London meeting of the Council of Foreign Ministers. Subsequently, under the treaty of 1942 the Japanese surrender obliged the Soviet Union to evacuate Iran by March 2, 1946. As a counter to these Soviet thrusts Bevin ostentatiously had consultations with all the British Middle Eastern diplomats, and the Regent of Greece was, also, in England at the time of the Council meeting.

Earlier disagreements about the satellite states were not settled at the London Conference. Bevin, faced by the demand for Soviet trusteeship of an Italian colony[2] (Tripoli-

---

[1] When the Soviet Union proposed at Potsdam that it be made trustee of one of the Italian colonies, Churchill said: "The British, of course, have great interests in the Mediterranean and any marked change in the status quo will need long and careful consideration." Byrnes, *Speaking Frankly* (New York, 1947), p. 76.

[2] Bevin later expressed his suspicions of the Soviet Union's desire "to come right across, shall I say, the throat of the British Commonwealth." *Parliamentary Debates*, House of Commons, Vol. 415, November 7, 1945, clmn. 1342. On one occasion during the Council meeting Bevin referred to a remark of Molotov as the most Hitler thing he had ever heard. Molotov started to leave and Bevin apologized. Dulles wrote: "Mr. Bevin was bluff and hearty, easily angered and quickly repentant of his anger. Mr. Molotov treated him as a banderillero treats a bull, planting darts that would arouse him to an outburst—from which he reacted in a manner implying a tendency to make concessions." John Foster Dulles, *War or Peace* (New York, 1950), p. 28; Byrnes, *Speaking Frankly*, pp. 94-96.

tania), rejected it with heat. A Cabinet meeting considered British policy. Britain had promised the Senussi of Cyrenaica that they would not again fall under Italian rule. In regard to Libya and Tripolitania, Bevin supported an American proposal that the Italian colonies be given their independence after a preparatory trusteeship under the United Nations. He also proposed that Eritrea and Somaliland be considered in connection with the provision of an outlet to the sea for Ethiopia.

Soviet demands for Italian reparations were resisted. Molotov revealed his hand when he told Bevin that the Soviet Union would be prepared for an early Italian Peace Conference, "if the United States agreed to an Allied Control Council for Japan."[3] At any rate, failing to secure concessions, Molotov was prepared to break up the meeting, and finally refused to approve even the protocol which would list the agreements concluded.

The harsh tactics and new demands of Molotov raised a dismal prospect. If there was to be no speedy peace, if the work of reconstruction was to be hampered, if the Russians were bent on expansionism, the British Government would have to make a sharp appraisal of its resources and of the positions it would have to hold.

The failure made public the disagreements and conflicts which had long been simmering behind the facade of Big Three Unity. This tardy revelation was salutary, but it also put Bevin at a disadvantage with left-wing members of his own Party. Presumably to reassure them he closed his Parliamentary account of the meeting with the letters of friendship which he and Molotov had exchanged.

In his public speeches Bevin did not and could not re-

---

[3]   Byrnes, *op. cit.*, p. 104.

pudiate the necessity of Big Three Unity.[4] But serious British opinion, and, I believe, subsequent British policy, were expressed in the following comment on the stalemate of the London meeting: "Failing inter-allied agreement, each individual ally will—indeed, must—carry on as he thinks best in those areas which he holds. Life and reconstruction can not wait. In this way, the London meeting has strongly, perhaps decisively, consolidated the division of Europe and the world into zones of influence."[5]

When the disagreement became known, the leftists were inclined to hold Bevin guilty, accusing him of maintaining

----

[4] He could only venture so far as to say: "I cannot accept the view that all my policy and the policy of His Majesty's Government must be based entirely on the Big Three." *Parliamentary Debates,* House of Commons, Vol. 416, Nov. 23, 1945, clmn. 762.

[5] "A Student of Europe" in *The Observer,* Sept. 30, 1945. Another characteristic comment sought to explain Russian actions as motivated by a search for security "in the self-sufficiency of a great land Power" rather than an "intimate collaboration of all the great victorious Powers in so administering the peace settlement that German military strength can never revive." The writer was prepared to recognize Russian objections to treating France and China as great powers. In meeting Soviet objections Britain, by acting as leader and "trustee" of the Commonwealth and small powers (including France), could talk on equal terms with the two Superpowers. "To western eyes it appears now obvious that a main buttress of European peace must be a close association of Powers led by Great Britain, with France as second member, including the kingdoms of Scandinavia and the Low Countries, eventually perhaps Portugal and a liberalized Italy, and having an eastern outpost in Greece; with a powerful friend across the Atlantic, the degree of whose future interest in purely European affairs remains problematic. Mr. Bevin, in the House of Commons on November 7, powerfully maintained that western Europe has as good a right as eastern to regional association. The argument is perfectly valid; but it is vital to the prospects of world peace that Great Britain acknowledge that the converse is equally true." Article, "The Schism of Europe," *The Round Table,* XXXVI (December, 1945), pp. 3-8. In a New York speech (Oct. 6, 1945), John Foster Dulles, adviser to Secretary Byrnes, said "that there would be no bloc of Western Powers, if the United States can avoid it," but he admitted that, if disagreement should continue, "it would lead to different nations carrying out their ideas in particular areas, which might not necessarily be a permanent disaster but would be most unfortunate." *The Times,* Oct. 8, 1945.

Tory policies. As a rule, the left wing of the Labour Party failed to allow for the competitive character of international politics and the tragically inescapable suspicions which haunt them. An editorial in the *New Statesman and Nation* revealed this failure in a very striking way. After blaming Bevin for following the principle of continuity in foreign policy [in this case, trying to keep the Soviets out of the Mediterranean], the editorial urged Bevin to declare that he would have no more of this maneuvering for positions of power. If that does not work, " a poor alternative—let us end this United Nations' sham, accept the splitting of the world into spheres, and agree to live unaggressively, though disunited inside our own back-yards."[6]

2. *Britain, the Two Superpowers and the United Nations.*

At Moscow in December, 1945, Secretary Byrnes proposed an unappreciated toast to Stalin. "Whom war hath joined together, let not peace put asunder."[7] Disunity now prevailed. The overriding facts were the prospective existence of a world organization, the United Nations, and the obvious absence of a world community.

In terms of power Britain could not qualify as an equal partner of the two Superpowers. There was, thus, an element of unreality in talk about the Big Three. The slogan of the unity of the Big Three became even more hollow. Still, this initial frustration could be thought of as a quarrel over the peace and not as the inadmissible possibility of a prelude to another war. Hopes were thwarted and continued to exist. Domestic political considerations and the absence of an alternative course, therefore, compelled Bevin

---

6 *New Statesman and Nation,* Sept. 22, 1945.

7 Byrnes, *op. cit.,* p. 118.

to continue to seek Big Three agreement and to pay lip service to it, while he attempted to hold on to such British positions as could be held. This necessitated a careful reduction of commitments and an attempted adjustment of Britain's relations with the Middle East and Asia. The urgency of this course increased with the gathering strength of Soviet opposition and with the progressive revelation of British weakness. Britain required a long and peaceful recuperative period. The magnitude of its economic problems was not adequately understood in Britain or the United States. Nor was there strength in Britain's neighbors on the European Continent, and Britain's recovery and political security were partly dependent on the revival of Western Europe.

Weakness and the lingering fog of war prevented Britain from embarking on a strong and independent foreign policy as the other members of the Big Three could do. The Soviet Union controlled the Balkans and menaced the Mediterranean and Middle East. The United States, whose officials remained reserved on the incipient cold war, presented problems of another order. Upon the end of the fighting against Japan, Lend-Lease was terminated. Britain was, therefore, confronted with the necessity of obtaining large dollar loans. For a considerable period Britain would have to import food and raw materials on credit. Even the speediest transition of British industries, overwhelmingly geared for war, to the making of export goods, and the rapid demobilization of the armed forces, could not free Britain from the necessity of borrowing. To cope with its shortages and weakness, Britain depended upon planning and controls. The United States, on the other hand, in the flush of its strength, was concerned with the removal of currency restrictions and the promotion of free trade. Britain had endorsed these aims in the Atlantic Charter and in the

Lend-Lease agreements, but their fullfillment presented challenges to the system of Imperial Preferences and serious difficulties in dealing with the sterling balances. American policy appeared to menace the protective restrictions of a debtor, and to the proponents of planning the United States began to loom as the caricature of boom-and-bust liberal capitalism.

During the war the British had vainly argued this issue of control with the United States. The British economist and Treasury representative, John Maynard Keynes, wrote that he was a "hopeless sceptic" about the return to nine-teenth century *laissez-faire* which the State Department ad-vocated. Keynes believed that future policy would require state trading in commodities, international cartels in impor-tant manufactures and quantitative restrictions on non-es-sential imports. In his mind these were necessary for an orderly economic life, and *laissez-faire* would outlaw them.[8]

Now Keynes, who thought of himself as a Liberal, was no isolated voice. His views on control were shared by the Labour Party and by many Conservatives. For example, the Conservative L. S. Amery, in advocating a European as-sociation or commonwealth based on mutual cooperation, attacked American economic policy as a nineteenth-century conception of promiscuous international trade within the framework of fixed exchanges and the most favored nation clause. Amery believed that this kind of policy, which would force Britain to abandon the Imperial Preference system, had brought on the Great Depression.[9]

The sudden termination of Lend-Lease (August 19, 1945) immediately compelled Britain to seek a loan from

---

[8] R. F. Harrod, *The Life of John Maynard Keynes* (New York, 1951), pp. 567-568.
[9] *The Times,* Nov. 27, 1945.

the United States. In negotiating the loan the British did not have the advantage of the later American fear of Russia. The stipulations of the loan, conceived in terms of assistance to a needy former ally, called for Britain's return to the free convertibility of the pound sterling and, after five years, repayment of principal with 2% interest over fifty years.[10]

In the British view, uncertainty seemed to be the great mark of the United States. The latter at first largely dissociated itself from the British position in Greece and was withdrawing from the Middle East. The large scale of its demobilization meant that the United States could offer no effective support in the minor skirmishes of power politics and even suggested the retirement of the United States into isolationism. The United States, while frowning on British Socialism, was anti-imperialist and anti-colonial. This side of American policy was revealed in criticism of British action in Indonesia and in protests against British peace negotiations with Thailand.

The United States also was far more prepared than Britain was to bargain for immediate conclusion of peace treaties. The anxiety frequently expressed by Secretary Byrnes, concerning the ill effects of Big Three discord and his obvious desire for definite treaties, increased the bargaining power of the Soviet Union. Disagreement with the Soviet Union reached the state of deadlock in the Balkan Allied Control Councils, and in Austria. In the face of this stalemate Britain was not ready for a new meeting of the Council of Foreign Ministers. The moves to resume negotiations, Harriman's interview with Stalin, and Byrnes' pro-

---

[10] R. F. Harrod, *The Life of John Maynard Keynes* (New York, 1951), pp. 586-623; Leisa Bronson and John C. Jackson, "The Anglo-American Financial and Trade Agreements," *Public Affairs Bulletin*, No. 41 (Washington, 1946).

posal of a meeting in Moscow, were American initiatives. The British Government probably shared the diplomat's objections, mentioned by Byrnes, and looked for some sign of Russian willingness to cooperate in dealing with urgent European problems before it would risk a further failure.[11]

The Moscow Conference in December, 1945, was held on the initiative of Secretary Byrnes, still in search of agreements with the Soviet Union and eager to clear the way for the first meetings of the Security Council and the General Assembly of the United Nations. Given Soviet intransigeance and the American desire for agreement, the results of the Conference were not surprising. The procedure for the European peace treaties with Finland, Italy and the satellite countries was specified in such a way as to save the faces of all concerned. The governments of Rumania and Bulgaria were to be broadened and then recognized. Britain had already secured U. S. consent to the participation of India, Australia and New Zealand in the Far Eastern Commission dealing with Japan. The Allied Council, meeting in Tokyo, also was open to them and to Russia and China. But the terms of the agreement did not obscure the fact that the occupation of Japan was to be an American show. After that Britain had no vital interest in Japan or Korea. The three Foreign Secretaries agreed that China needed a unified Chinese government with participation by democratic elements in all branches of the National Government. The Moscow Conference ratified existing realities, and in the subsequent peace treaty negotiations with Italy and the satellite states, the decisive factor was who controlled them. Where

---

[11] Byrnes, *op. cit.*, pp. 108-109. Notice the emphasis in Byrnes' account of Potsdam; "Nevertheless, we believed our agreement on reparations enabled us to avoid denouncing their unilateral action in removing people and property from their zone." *Ibid.*, p. 87.

there were divided battlegrounds, as in Austria and Germany, there were no peace treaties. Disputed borderlands, Iran and Greece, were to be a source of constant quarreling.

The first meeting of the United Nations in London became the forum for these disputes. The British approach to the United Nations was more cautious than the American. The use of the atomic bomb in Japan had shaken the British, and in the House of Commons debate on the United Nations' Charter, many members expressed their doubts about the adequacy of the organization for the atomic age. In speaking to the Preparatory Commission of the United Nations Bevin agreed that many of the assumptions of San Francisco would have to be revised, although he considered the proponents of immediate world government to be unwise. "As I see it, the idea of world government is something which must be carefully nursed in order that the right atmosphere may be created. It is not something that can be imposed from the top, but must be the result of a period of growth. . . . After all, nations have been formed by history . . . it is perhaps not surprising that I myself should hold that the limitations of heredity can to some extent be corrected by cooperation and environment."[12]

When the United Nations met in London, the British Prime Minister rose to the hopes of the occasion in saying that the United Nations, unlike the League of Nations, must become the overriding factor in foreign policy.[13] Later, Bevin fell in with the spirit of the occasion and, particularly, welcomed the Security Council's Military Staff Committee and the Atomic Commission.[14] These happy sentiments soon yielded to bitter debates on the presence of British troops

---

[12] *The Times,* Aug. 17, 1945.
[13] *The Times,* Jan. 11, 1946.
[14] *The Times,* Jan. 18, 1946.

in Greece and Syria and charges of imperialism against Britain and the Soviet Union.

A minor survival of Big Three unity persisted in relation to Spain. On the Continent there was still a tendency to think of Franco's government as a survival of the Fascist era. France and the Soviet Union championed this view. Bevin firmly announced his government's dislike of Franco's dictatorship, but he was even more emphatic in saying that a change in Spain was up to the Spanish people. Only reluctantly did the British Government eventually accept the United Nations' resolution and recall its Ambassador from Spain.

3. Germany: *The Spoils of Victory.*

Germany, expected to be the incentive for Big Three Unity, became a major stage of conflict. The Allied Control Council, established at Potsdam, providing the framework for unity, was the cockpit for a struggle which periodically shifted to the meetings of the Foreign Ministers. The British position in Germany involved great difficulties. They held the most industrialized areas, and these, especially the Ruhr, were the most devastated and most dependent. Thus, at Potsdam, the British were greatly concerned about Germany's eastern boundary, for they wanted Germany to retain the eastern agricultural districts and to be able to reduce the importation of food.[15]

French objections to establishing central organs of government in Germany until the Ruhr and Rhineland had been arranged to the satisfaction of France, initially frustrated Four Power accord. France's action served to mask the unilateral Russian policy of wholesale removals of machinery and the Sovietization of eastern Germany. The argu-

---

[15] Lucius D. Clay, *Decision in Germany* (Garden City, 1950), p. 39.

ment that fear of German aggression would promote Big Three Unity lost its force in the face of the devastation of German cities. For a brief time, at any rate, Germany could not commit aggression, whereas Soviet actions injured Britain and engendered suspicion. For the British, Germany was a momentary liability, whereas the Soviet Union could ruthlessly exploit its zone. Food did not come from the east. Britain and the United States were compelled to import food for Germany.

The British-held Ruhr presented formidable problems. Although Britain itself was hard pressed for food, the Ruhr coal mines could not be placed in operation without importing food supplies. By October 2, 1945, the British Commander in Germany, Marshal Montgomery, was expressing fears about the coming winter. The British government was early convinced that German economic life had to be salvaged not so much for the sake of Germany as for the sake of Europe. But it did not devise the means of achieving this essential end.[16]

The hopes of unity, however, were not immediately dispelled in all quarters. German affairs, at first, were largely in the hands of the military, who tried to ignore political questions and to devote their energies to the urgent problems of establishing order and relieving famine. American policy was in the short run less flexible than British policy. American officials were particularly impatient with French obstructionism. When the United States proposed that Britain, Russia and the United States go ahead in Germany without

---

[16] While American observers, Senator Kilgore, Judge Rosenman, Crowley, and William Clayton were impressed by the vast surviving potential of German industry, a characteristic British view was: "Germany must again become a productive economic society. Or else, either the German people must be kept alive by Allied charity, or the whole country will become a great area of famine and pestilence—and epidemics do not recognize frontiers." W. N. Ewer in *Daily Herald,* July 20, 1945.

France, Britain objected.[17] Britain assumed a mediatory role between France and the United States, a role which she often essayed in later Franco-American conflicts over Germany.

The bewildering rapidity of the transition from the termination of one war to a cold war among the victors, painfully impressed the British. Scarcity of food upset their original plan of drawing food from their German zone.[18] In July it was evident that food would have to be imported into Germany.[19] On December 12, 1945, the British Control Commission sharply curtailed military food purchases in Germany.[20] During November and December, 1945, 112,-000 tons of United States' wheat, intended for British consumption, and 50,000 tons of potatoes from British stores went to Germany.[21]

The horrors of the German vacuum mocked the planners and policy-makers. The American economic advisers to the Office of Military Government reported in September, 1945 that the Potsdam formula for the collection of reparations and for industrial disarmament of Germany, would be very difficult to fulfill. The report of this group, headed by Calvin Hoover, had reached the British by September 17. The report had taken 74% of the German diet of 1932 as a minimum standard. Even that could not be maintained by a Germany deprived of its eastern food-producing area and with a larger population, if Germany had to pay occupation costs and reparations and endure industrial disarmament.

[17] J. B. Hynd, the Chancellor of the Duchy of Lancaster, in a speech at Sheffield. *The Observer,* Dec. 9, 1945. The Labour Party's paper, *Daily Herald,* Dec. 10, 1945, headlined the speech "Britain Refuses to Snub France."

[18] *The Times,* May 16, 1945.

[19] *New York Times,* July 24, 1945.

[20] *The Times,* December 13, 1945. By March 26, 1946, British troops in Germany were forbidden to purchase food of any kind.

[21] *News Chronicle,* November 12, 1945.

The report insisted that if some industries were destroyed, others would have to be expanded.[22] In the discussions on the level of German industry during the last months of 1945, the British proposed a much higher steel level (9,000,000 tons) than even Calvin Hoover thought necessary for sustaining the German economy. Hoover's estimate was 7,800,-000 tons, but, according to General Clay, a State Department memorandum had suggested to Clay that three and one half million tons would be adequate.[23]

Britain was concerned to keep the German economy viable, but she was, also, eager to destroy Germany's shipping resources. This second aim, which was followed in the later destruction of the port facilities of Kiel and Hamburg, and in the destruction of shipbuilding yards, aroused a great bitterness among the Germans, who saw the policy for what it was and ignored the relatively benevolent work of the British occupation force in the early restoration of German production. Britain was also prepared to take reparations from Germany in order to restore Britain's industrial production. The Board of Trade requested British Trade Associations to compile lists of the plants and machinery which their members desired to obtain from Germany. They were urged not to overlook the possibility of taking somewhat worn equipment pending delivery of new British equipment.[24]

The gravity of the problems arising from the division of Germany was not immediately appreciated, for there were

---

[22] Raymond Daniell in *New York Times,* October 8, 1945.

[23] L. Clay, *Decision in Germany,* p. 108. Edwin Pauley in New York attacked those who wanted to restore German industry. *New York Herald Tribune,* October 12, 1945. The "man-eating civilians" still had a loud voice at the time. The phrase is from *The Chicago Daily News,* October 22, 1945.

[24] *The Observer,* November 4, 1945. *The Observer* was opposed to private industry seeking reparations on the ground that European recovery might be jeopardized. British use of Helgoland as a bombing area later became a powerful irritant in Anglo-German relations.

43

great stocks of raw materials available for the factories. But the division of Germany, whereby the British Zone was cut off from raw materials and food, kept production in the British Zone (1946 and first quarter of 1947) to about one fourth of the 1936 output.[25] Very little dismantling was done in the British Zone until after the first year of occupation. By that time the Americans had stopped. When the British began in the midst of economic distress, the proceedings were very unpopular and added both economic and psychological obstacles to production.[26]

These difficulties were intensified by another. If the British Zone could not trade with Eastern Germany, then the industrial power of Germany would have to compete directly with Britain in European markets. As the alternative to this was German disintegration, the British dilemma seemed to offer no way out. The coal supply, however, was desperately short, and the British were not inhibited from encouraging German coal production.

Britain subordinated denazification to the requirements of production. The directors of the Rhine Westphalian coal syndicate were not rounded up until coal production had been resumed and had reached in November the level of 30% of pre-war production.[27] Before the war the North

---

[25] W. Friedmann, *The Allied Military Government of Germany* (London, 1947), pp. 189-192, 196-201.

[26] As the British Zone was the industrial area, most of the dismantling took place there. Of 1,198,000 tons of material collected for reparation, 989,000 tons came from the British Zone. Britain in maintaining the dismantling policy after the United States had abandoned it sought to further its own interest while also satisfying French demands. See M. J. Bonn, "The British in Germany," *The Fortnightly Review* (November, 1950), 292-298.

[27] Not until the British "North German Coal Control" had its fingers on all the levers and was able to dispense with the Krupps and others, were they finally taken into custody. "The delay was an administrative precaution." W. N. Ewer in *Daily Herald*, November 28, 1945. In June, 1945, the daily output of coal was about 40,000 tons as compared with a daily average of 385,000 tons in 1936. *Daily Telegraph*, June 22, 1945.

German coal industry employed 337,000 workers. In July, 1945, there were only 133,350 workers available. A vigorous effort to find coal miners among German prisoners and to recruit young men followed. By March 1, 1946, 76,000 more had been found. In July, weekly clean coal output was 374,-000 tons. In February, the weekly average was more than 1,000,000 tons.[28] Increased coal production meant exports to promote the industrial recovery of Europe.

By the end of April, 1946, the British Control Commission took over from the military. Meanwhile, Britain had had to use dollars to buy wheat for Germany, and substantial food cuts were made on March 4. The coal production for the week ending March 11, dropped 10%.[29] In May, Herbert Morrison again went to Washington to consult about the food situation, especially in Germany. The continued drain caused by the obligations of occupation amounted to £80,000,000 for 1946. This meant, so some critics said, that Britain was paying reparations to Germany. The financial difficulties of Britain caused the British to adopt occupation policies which irritated other European states. For instance, countries to which the British Occupation Zone sent exports, were asked for payment in dollars.[30]

A Zonal Advisory Council of Germans was set up in January and local elections were held. British plans envisaged the promotion of German Socialism, which would have nationalized the major industries of the British Zone. Late in November 1946, the German Socialist leader, Kurt Schumacher, visited London on the invitation of the British Labour Party. In June, Bevin also proposed that Germany be organized on a federal basis, though he had also proposed

---

[28]   *Manchester Guardian,* March 22, 1946.
[29]   *Manchester Guardian,* March 22, 1946.
[30]   *Financial Times,* December 4, 1945.

that the Ruhr be internationalized. On June 19,1946, Schumacher announced to a Berlin press conference that the British-appointed provincial councils were completing plans for the socializing of German industry. Another feature of the program involved breaking up the large estates in the British Zone.[31]

A plan to take over the Vereinigte Stahlwerke in the Ruhr was delayed as a result of the Paris discussions of the Ruhr and Rhineland.[32] Criticisms of wasteful administration constantly plagued Chancellor Hynd, whose headquarters at Norfolk House was christened "Hyndquarters." British policy in Germany finally stalled before the magnitude of problems for which British resources were inadequate. In the spring of 1946 the economic problems drove the American Military Government to consider the fusion of the American Zone with any other zones of occupation. This could only mean the British Zone. At Paris in July, 1946, Bevin had stated that the British government had to take steps to protect the British taxpayer, for the British governmen was spending £80,000,000 a year on Germany. This expenditure was largely being made to restore industrial production, designed to meet European requirements.[33]

The fusion of the two zones was at first limited to economic matters. General arrangements were agreed upon during the summer, but hard bargaining went on in Washington in November when the respective shares of the financial responsibility of the occupying powers were discussed. The British were held to a fifty-fifty share, although they

---

[31] *New York Herald Tribune,* June 20, 1946. Bevin indicated an intention to support nationalization on February 21, 1946, October 22, 1946, and August 4, 1947.

[32] *Daily Telegraph,* August 12, 1946.

[33] Clay, *op. cit.,* p. 167.

had asked for less. Financial support for the Bizonal Economic Council was aimed at restoring German productivity and advancing exports to the point where the Bizone would be self-supporting. The target for 1947 was not achieved and in the British Zone the bulk of exports were coal and timber. The greatest manufacturing area of Europe was reduced almost to the colonial position of an exporter of raw materials.[34] Apart from the basic problem of providing food, the German manufacturer had little incentive to export, because he was paid in unrealistic and largely useless marks. Barter on the black market brought something tangible. But currency reform was, as yet, too ticklish a subject to handle.

Fusion made German policy even more a matter of foreign policy. Early in 1947 the Government began considering the transfer of complete responsibility for German policy to the Foreign Office. The decision was taken in April, 1947, and Frank Pakenham succeeded J. B. Hynd as Chancellor of the Duchy of Lancaster (the ministry entrusted with German affairs).[35]

The British plan to move in the direction of nationalization was slowed down for various reasons. First of all, it would have added a controversial element to the difficulties of fusion. Secondly, Bevin was prepared to wait until the Moscow Conference (March, 1947) before taking such a decisive step without the agreement of all the occupying powers. British financial weakness increased so that negotiations for the assumption by the United States of almost complete financial responsibility for the trade and fuel of the Bizone were concluded by the fall of 1947. Thereafter, the

---

[34] *Manchester Guardian,* August 16, 1947. Moreover, Germany had imported timber before the war and the British Zone was very poor in timber. *The Times,* Aug. 30, 1947.

[35] *Times,* April 18, 1947; *Daily Telegraph,* April 18, 1947; *Daily Mail,* April 29, 1947.

view of the United States had predominance. By this time, also, the United States was concerned with associating Germans in their own government. It could be argued plausibly that nationalization was an issue to be decided by the Germans themselves and not by the occupying powers.

4. *The Shadow of Facts and the Flicker of Hope.*

Reviewing foreign affairs on June 4, 1946, Mr. Bevin emphasized the necessity of great power agreement and cooperation. He recalled the earlier grounds for cooperation, opposition to Nazism, and urged its validity as a basis for the future. Yet he did this in order to underscore the difficulties caused by Russia. "The only thing that will block understanding is if any of us develop exclusive power politics, and do not use our perfectly legitimate interests in a way that will, as I said at the beginning, ultimately merge into a world security scheme."[36] In respect to the issues which he discussed, the Soviet Union appeared as the disturber of the peace. He approved the United States proposal for a twenty-five year treaty to insure the disarmament of Germany,[37] and could not understand Soviet opposition. "I will not admit failure yet. We will try again." But . . . "we cannot be forced to acquiesce in an indefinite stalemate." He favored French interest in the Saar, but for the Ruhr envisaged an international control.[38]

---

[36] *Weekly Hansard,* House of Commons, No. 19, June 4, 1946, clmns. 1835, 1833-1858.

[37] Soviet oposition probably arose from a recognition that this meant an unwelcome readiness of the United States to participate in European affairs.

[38] This speech is genuinely a Foreign Office production, which states policy in terms of Bevin's own difficulties in the Labour Party. Bevin himself stated that he would stick very closely to his brief. Its purport was to announce "another effort at agreement before deciding on any final alternative course." A *Times* leader observed: "Both sides are and must be profoundly reluctant to accept the logic of disagreement." *The Times,* June 5, 1946.

Bevin was pleased that the views of ex-enemy states were to be heard at the Peace Conference. He was rather ingenuous, however, about the actual achievements. The countries in the Russian orbit, after all, received such justice as the Soviet Union wished. Similarly, Italy, apart from Trieste and the reparations question, was dealt with as Britain and the United States proposed. The most severe bargaining took place over an area, Trieste, where the two zones of influence met. In regard to Trieste, Bevin professed that British policy there favored a solution based on ethnic rather than strategic principles.[39] Germany, he continued, posed the real problem and opportunity of European peace.[40] He listed the possibilities of European organization: (1) a balance between states of equal strength; (2) domination by one power or by two blocs of powers; (3) united effort by the Four Powers with the cooperation of their smaller allies. This listing represents the confusion of bankruptcy, for at the moment the first two courses were not feasible. Thus Bevin favored the third approach. In the United Nations, Britain's role would not be that of an intermediary between Russia and the United States. Britain stood on an equal footing with those powers.

In spite of Bevin's efforts to reassure the Labour Party

---

[39] *Weekly Hansard,* House of Commons, No. 29, Oct. 22, 1946, clmns. 1509-1510, 1493-1528. Strategic considerations were inescapable. Bevin constantly insisted that Palestine be considered as a part of the Middle Eastern problem.

[40] The following is a good example of Bevin's labored whistling in the dark. "If, therefore, we take Mr. Byrnes' pledge of American cooperation, Marshal Stalin's words, the declaration which I have just made of Great Britain's desire for four power cooperation, and the known willingness of France to collaborate in European security, and if this desire for cooperation can be applied in practice in the conference room, and written into the settlement, the future of Europe looks brighter than it has for ages." *Ibid.,* clmn. 1517.

malcontents, they persisted in their fears that the continuity of British policy meant a breach with Russia, association with the United States and the maintenance of heavy military expenses. They feared, correctly, that Churchill's Fulton and Zurich speeches, which proposed Anglo-American association and European Union, based on a reconciliation of Germany and France, forecast the future of British policy. After the Republican victory in the Congressional elections in 1946 and while Bevin was in New York, their parliamentary members presented a protest against Bevin's policy. Although the protest finally was not brought to a vote, the Party leadership was worried.

5. *Socialist Foreign Policy: Reductio Ad Absurdum.*

Before the heavy winter (1946-47) revealed further British weakness, Bevin spoke with some confidence of what had been achieved and of the future. The troubles of the world were blamed less on the Soviet Union than on the destructiveness of the war. He was concerned to remedy the abuse of the veto in the Security Council and to create political conditions of such a character that armaments would become unnecessary and the United Nations would be made the basis of Britain's relationship with the world. The war had left only two great powers, the Soviet Union and the United States. "Great Britain lies midway in geography and way of life . . . I believe we have entered the first stage of establishing concord and harmony between the Great Powers." All of his decisions were taken in relation to the prosperity of the common people. Thus, "we must avoid the creation of a cesspool of cheap and half-starved labour in Middle Europe." Elsewhere in the world, where Britain was free to act, it had followed "our pacificatory and modernizing course." Britain had tied herself to no power and deals with "every problem on its merits."[41]

Mr. Bevin's assurances were not wholly effective. During the first four months of 1947, British ministers made the rounds of Britain, explaining British Foreign Policy to private meetings of Labour Party conferences.[42]

In 1946 and 1947 the emptiness of a Socialist policy became clear in a multitude of writings and discussions. The supporters of a Socialist foreign policy usually assumed either that it was possible to inaugurate international relations anew with a general declaration of universal benevolence or that Britain could withdraw from the international power struggle.

G. D. H. Cole, a prominent Labour writer on political and economic problems, argued that Britain should accept the waning of its power, concentrate on its own development, and within those limits strengthen democratic Socialism especially in Western Europe. Unfortunately, when Socialist parties take over governments, international relations do go on as before. Free elections and democratic gradualism compel Socialist governments to maintain many things which they do not like. The reason for this is that "they are acting consciously within the principle of continuity, and are not prepared for a revolutionary repudiation, as not binding them, of everything that happened before they took office."

---

[41] *The Times,* Dec. 23, 1946. This broadcast speech was less a statement of policy than an explanation of it to appease a troubled people. Strangely enough, *The Times* said that Bevin rightly was satisfied with the results of his perseverance. "There have been too many voids left by the war and too eager competition to fill them. Now not only are some of these beginning to be filled by a process of natural growth, but the Great Powers have had time to test each other, and to find that none of them can have things all its own way." The test for the future was Germany. True, earlier arrangements had called for a delay in the German treaty. "Most of them were based, as time has proved, on an overestimate of international morality and of the power of the victors to control events." *The Times,* Dec. 23, 1946.

[42] *The Times,* Jan. 8 and 9, 1947.

Cole branded Soviet Communism as Trotskyism and called for a Western European Socialist Union. This European Union would be directed not against the Soviet Union but only against the dark forces of the west. The union would be entirely preoccupied with home problems. "As for military affairs, I do not want Western unity to be involved in them in any way."[43]

Harold Laski, addressing the Labour Party's conference, suggested that Socialist governments should not mistrust each other. "Let capitalist governments mistrust one another; that mistrust is inherent in capitalist society. But governments like the Russian and our own, are the surest hope of peace when they find the road to the same ends and combine their strength to fight whatever dangers they encounter on the way. . . . The common people, both in Great Britain and in Russia, have the right, based upon a massive experience, to say to their leaders that cooperation is the alternative to destruction."[44]

Late in 1946 the Fabian International Research group, in which the leftists were well represented, began an inquiry into "the outlines of a Socialist Foreign Policy for Great Britain." The result of the Committee's discussion was a pamphlet, "Foreign Policy: the Labour Party's Dilemma." Leonard Woolf, once so clear in his call for a Socialist for-

---

[43] Cole, "On Labour's Foreign Policy" (London, 1946). In 1948 Cole again looked for the mediation of a Socialist Europe between the extreme views of the Soviet Union and the United States and added: "How this can be brought about I do not profess to know with any clarity." Cole, "Europe and the Problem of Democracy," Peace Aims Pamphlet, No. 44 (London, 1948), p. 12.

[44] *Report of the 45th Conference of the Labour Party* (London, 1946), p. 106. In a later lecture, Laski again affirmed his faith in an undefined Socialist foreign policy, which alone could promote a federal world order. Laski, "Socialism as Internationalism," Fabian Research Series, No. 132 (London, 1949).

eign policy, had to report that "the relation between Social-ism and the question of foreign policy is nearly always re-mote and obscure." Woolf's conclusions, presented as a sum-mary of the discussions, were that the objectives of British foreign policy for the next few years would have to be peace and collective security; but he admitted that these were not specifically Socialist. Woolf urged that in international af-fairs Britain should be impartial, not neutral. Britain had become a second class power and must recognize the fact; yet it must work for a free and peaceful world and avoid the power politics of the United States and the Soviet Union. But the pamphlet was even more unusual, for it carried a critical note on Woolf by W. N. Ewer, the diplomatic cor-respondent of the Labour Party paper, the *Daily Herald,* and an introduction by Harold Laski who disagreed with both of the writers, for against Woolf he maintained that there was a Socialist foreign policy and against Ewer he charged that Ewer's power politics and espousal of coopera-tion with the United States involved the same principles as those of Lord Vansittart or of Sir Eyre Crowe.[45]

As the British economic position in the first half of 1947 finally appeared in all its weakness and with American pol-icy still limited to the Truman Doctrine a group of leftists

---

[45] *Fabian Publications: Research Series,* No. 121 (London, 1947), pp. 3, 7-9, 13. Rita Hinden, who was a member of the Fabian International Bureau, reviewing the pamphlet, criticized the timidity and naivete of Woolf and the dangerous power politics of Ewer, and, without mentioning Laski, obviously disagreed with him. Her conclusion was: "In the anarchy of the present world we cannot—unless we plump for neutrality—simply contract out of power politics—detest it as we may. Yet Socialists must inject some other element into their foreign policy as well. They must, wherever possible, apply in international conflicts, the principles of justice and agreement, rather than arbitrariness and force. As Big Power strife intensifies, this is becoming more and more difficult. Herein lies our dilemma; the search for a foreign policy which solves it has only just begun." *Socialist Commentary,* XIII (1948), 81-83.

issued (May 1) their statement of policy in a pamphlet, "Keep Left." Largely the work of Richard Crossman, Ian Mikardo and Michael Foot, "Keep Left" demanded the abandonment of the "Tory idea of bolstering up the British Empire with American dollars and fighting America's battle with British soldiers." It opposed any sphere of influence and, to prevent such a division of Europe and the world, called for the closely associated endeavors of France and the British Commonwealth.

Proponents of a Socialist foreign policy had little to offer except that presumably the British Empire should not be bolstered up. For the harsh days of 1946-47 this was less than Mr. Bevin was offering. After the frustration of peace and the advent of the Cold War, after the wartime efforts to win Soviet good will and cooperation, a policy which envisaged unilateral British benevolence to win Soviet good will and a demonstration of British impotence appeared to be little more than a gaily colored but unlighted candle held up against a darkly oppressive sky.[46]

---

[46] In a later pamphlet, Crossman agreed that Britain had more in common with the United States than with Russia and argued against the purists of the left that the Atlantic Pact "is not something dirty and distasteful for Socialists, but a necessity of survival." R. H. Crossman and Kenneth Younger, "Socialist Foreign Policy," Fabian Tract, No. 287 (London, 1951).

CHAPTER THREE

The Reduction of Commitments

"England cannot afford to be little."
William Huskisson

The War severely tested the British Commonwealth of sovereign states and the more dependent Empire. The latter had, also, been promised a gradual development of self-government. During the War, Canada, Australia and New Zealand increasingly looked for their security to the United States. The states of the Commonwealth formed an admirable community, a wholesome association, which by its voluntary character could not coordinate policy or concentrate power except in time of war. Its flexibility defied human logic and permitted wonderful devices to meet new situations, for the actual Commonwealth is "the mere project of a Commonwealth, masquerading as the *societas perfecta.*"[1] A Colonial Development Plan, calling for heavy capital investment and the acceleration of the production of primary goods, was inaugurated during the War and extended by the Labour Government. Nigeria and, notably, the Gold Coast advanced towards constitutional life and self-government. But, elsewhere, tremendous forces menaced British imper-

---

[1] W. K. Hancock, *Survey of British Commonwealth Affairs.* Vol. I (New York, 1937), p. 490. See the excellent article by Karl Dietrich Erdmann. "Wandlungen des britischen Reichsbewusstseins vom 19. zum 20. Jahrhundert," *Saeculum,* II (1951), 595-617.

ial positions. In three areas long under the *Pax Britannica,* Southeast Asia, the Middle East and the Eastern Mediterranean, Britain was compelled to abandon positions. Unable to master the forces of Arab and Asian nationalism, Britain sought adjustments which might hold off an apparently unfathomable tide. The Labour Party was opposed to maintaining the Empire by force. It is a nice, and, possibly, a significant coincidence that when Britain did not have adequate force, her government was in the hands of a Party committed to abandon imperial rule.

1. *Southeast Asia: From Master to Partner.*

In 1942 Britain had offered self-government to India. This wartime offer was irrevocable, for victory in war did not increase Britain's strength. Not only was Britain unable to hold India, but she had become a debtor to India. In Burma and Malaya Britain had been defeated by the Japanese. Even though these territories were reoccupied, the imperial facade had been shattered. British imperial prestige could not recover from this collapse.[2] Far to the north the United States was supreme in Japan and Russia loomed in northern China.[3] Below these areas stretched Southeast Asia and

---

[2] "Nothing could have done more harm to British prestige than the prompt collapse of defences which we had sworn would be maintained. The defensive arrangements of Hong Kong were but a gesture in the gigantic system of bluff which took the place of a genuine fabric of defence in the eastern Empire. . . . British leaders . . . assured subject peoples that the greatest boon which they gained from their membership of the Empire was the security guaranteed to them by British might. These things were not merely said, but believed. The leaders and people of the British Empire bluffed themselves even more successfully than they bluffed others." H. V. Hodson, *Twentieth-Century Empire* (London, 1948), p. 49.

[3] The major British interest in China was property and investments (including Chinese bonds) which may have amounted to £177,000,000. A. S. B. Olver "Outline of British Policy in East and Southeast Asia, 1945-May, 1950," United Kingdom Paper No. 1, Eleventh (Lucknow) Conference of the Insti-

India, still at some distance from the spheres of influence of the two Superpowers. Here, the great problem was the urgent need for economic reconstruction and development. If this area remained sheltered from the intrusion of the Big Powers, a policy of promoting economic reconstruction and development had some chance of success. Malaya, Hong Kong, Borneo and Burma were reoccupied. Immediately, the problems were the restoration of a minimum of trade and the allotment of the exceedingly scarce food supplies. Burma, principal rice exporter for the area, had been the battleground of two successive campaigns. The failure of the monsoon further reduced the area's food sources. As late as 1948 Burma was exporting only one third of the quantity of rice which she had supplied before the war.

The economic interests of Britain in Southeast Asia were considerable: investments, business companies and shipping. These could not be protected by direct imperial control. The very protection of these interests required a policy which in promoting the economic reconstruction of the area would also ensure stability and the security of British holdings.

British policy in Southeast Asia, therefore, was hitched to the cause of Asian nationalism and had overtones of the fashionable welfare state. As Bevin put it to the Commons: "in the light of the independence movement all over this territory, which must be faced, and which we do not intend to frustrate, there had to be a guaranteed policy."[4] To replace

---

tute of Pacific Relations (London, 1950). In the Treaty of 1943, by which Britain waived her extra-territorial jurisdiction in China, she also abandoned her claim to take part in Chinese coastal trade and inland navigation. Chinese insistence on excluding the British from the coastal trade and the Civil War prevented any expansion of British trading interests in China itself.

[4] *Weekly Hansard,* House of Commons, No. 5, Feb. 21, 1946, clmn. 1363.

the centralizing influence of the Southeast Asia Command, and to coordinate the Southeast Asian policies of the India, Colonial and Foreign offices, Lord Killearn was appointed (Feb. 18, 1946) Chief Commissioner, South East Asia. In a characteristically obscure statement Bevin looked ahead: "There is Indonesia, Malaya, Ceylon, and a new China emerging. There is all that new development, and I think the policy we have to follow so far as the dependent territories are concerned which are emerging into independence, is to nurse them, guide them, help them to change over as a going concern, to keep their administration intact, to provide them with experts. I am not too sure that from the point of view of our own interests in this country, we should not do far better by helping these countries and assisting them from a purely trade point of view in trade and commerce than we did under the old fashioned Colonial system of the past. That is our policy for the Far East."[5] Inevitably, this policy was more a statement of desirable objectives than one which could be intensively carried out. Britain did provide some funds for reconstruction and aided in the restoration of communications and transportation in Siam and Burma. She advanced credits to Burma, in part, to finance Burmese nationalization of British interests. But a very large part of her contribution was in the form of using unrequited exports for paying off the sterling balances to Asian countries.

After the Japanese Armistice, the realities of Southeast Asia soon intruded. For their return to this area the British were initially unprepared in two ways. First of all, little planning had been done. Although the British Government was disposed to look favorably on Asian independence

---

5   *Ibid.*, clmns. 1363-1364.

movements, its agents were as ill-informed about the area as the Dutch and French were. It had been out of contact with Malaya and the East Indies for three years. Some British prisoners, interned in Java, perceived the changed conditions and temper, but they could not communicate their information.[8]

Secondly, the Japanese collapse found the British preparing a large scale invasion of Malaya. With the signing of the Japanese Armistice the Southwest Pacific Command came to an end, and the largely British Southeast Asia Command had already been entrusted with military responsibility for such areas as Burma and Indonesia. Thus Mountbatten's Command at Ceylon was commissioned to accept the surrender of the Japanese forces in Indonesia.[7] This change of duty was to be a surprising experience, highlighting the difficulties which Britain was to face in Southeast Asia.

a. INDONESIA

Now the Indonesian nationalists had been encouraged by the Japanese, who in preparation for their surrender had turned over arms to the nationalists. These, expecting the

---

6 Barbara Whittingham-Jones has written: "In London it was a constant grievance among those charged with responsibility for our Far Eastern interests that, after the fall of Singapore, Mr. Churchill would not allow its name to be mentioned in his presence." *The Contemporary Review,* No. 1023 (March, 1951), p. 187.

7 For the confusion attendant upon the change, see H. J. Van Mook, *The Stakes of Democracy in Southeast Asia* (New York, 1950), pp. 173-175. Of later developments the author adds: "The greatest harm caused by these high-handed proceedings was not so much the friction it caused between the British and the Dutch on the spot. For again it was one of the paradoxes of this story that the same anxiety to avoid commitments in a thorny situation, which made the British act with such ill-judged rashness, made them extend a very active and liberal aid to the Dutch in the training and equipping of forces that could relieve them of their duty." *Ibid.,* p. 188.

Americans, had put up posters with quotations from the Declaration of Independence and Lincoln. The English, unprepared for the assignment, did not land forces until Sept. 29. These troops, under Lieutenant General P. A. Christison had three directives: to disarm and send home the Japanese: to release and assist prisoners of war and interned civilians; and to preserve law and order until the Dutch could take over. But the Indonesian Republic had been proclaimed on August 17, and General Christison was in a cruel dilemma. He could not simply crush the Republic. He could not, however, recognize it without alienating Britain's ally, the Netherlands, and without adding strength to the swelling anti-imperialist forces all over Asia. The British General had insufficient forces, and, in addition, there were among them, British Indian troops. Indian Nationalists bitterly criticized this use of the British Indian troops in Indonesia.[8]

The Indonesian nationalists held most of Java, apart from Batavia. On Oct. 28, 1945, they attacked British forces at the naval base of Soerabaya. When the nationalists continued fighting to prevent the return of Dutch troops, the British were driven to use Japanese troops against them. The British thereby aroused a world scandal, and, of course, won the approval of neither the Dutch nor the Indonesians. Britain, however, was not minded to use force to maintain the empire of another power. From the middle of October British diplomacy was devoted to promoting a conference be-

---

[8] The first Dutch reaction to the Indonesian Republic was to consider it an insignificant gesture of Japanese collaborationists. The Political Manifesto of Soetan Sjahrir (who was not a collaborationist) blamed the Dutch for the helplessness of the Javanese before Japan and recognized that the "feeling of national awareness was also sharpened by the Japanese propaganda for pan-Asianism." Parts of this text are reproduced as an appendix in Charles Wolf, Jr., *The Indonesian Story* (New York, 1948).

tween the Dutch and Indonesians. Early the following year Sir Archibald Clark Kerr was sent to Java in order to persuade the nationalists and Dutch authorities to make a settlement. On January 21, 1946, the Soviet Ukraine brought the case to the Security Council as a threat to world peace. Finally, under British pressure, for British troops were to evacuate the islands by the end of November, 1946, the Dutch initialled the draft agreement of Linggadji, which gave *de facto* recognition to the Indonesian government. During this period, however, the British also trained and equipped the Dutch Army which took over part of Java.

b. THAILAND

The Indonesian affair, to Thailand's benefit, complicated the making of peace with Thailand. The location of their country between British Burma and French Indo-China had taught the Siamese pliability and the necessity of dividing her enemies. Before Pearl Harbor Thailand[9] had taken Laos and Cambodia from France, and after Pearl Harbor, declaring war on Britain and the United States (January 25, 1942), had taken at Japanese hands parts of Malaya and Burma. Although the United States had refused to recognize the Thai declaration of war, Britain had done so. Meanwhile, the Thai Ambassador in Washington headed a Free Thai movement opposed to the War, and Pridi, the Siamese Regent, was in charge of the movement. In this miracle of "facing both ways" the Siamese resistance had been instructed by Allied military authorities to refrain from open warfare against Japan.

In preparation for an occupation of Thailand, pending continued war against Japan, a twenty-one point military

---

[9] On June 12, 1940 Thailand concluded non-aggression treaties with Britain and France.

agreement had been prepared for the Allies. These terms were discussed in Washington, where some objections were raised. Then, when the Japanese surrender was imminent, Thailand on August 16 repudiated the declaration of war and expressed a willingness to restore British territory and to make reparations for damage to British and American property.[10]

A Siamese delegation travelled to Kandy, Ceylon, and there on September 8 signed a preliminary military agreement, providing for the entry of British troops into Thailand. Then the difficulties in Indonesia drew the British negotiators away from Siamese affairs. This delay enabled the Siamese to attempt to play the United States against Britain. The Siamese represented British demands for the maintenance of earlier trade treaties and for Siamese participation in the International Tin Cartel as oppressive imperialism. Ably assisted by American O.S.S. officers and a general lack of information, the Siamese caused the United States to ask for a delay in the negotiations. The formal agreement terminating the state of war was not signed until January 1, 1946.[11]

Actually, Siam was in a good bargaining position, for the country did have stores of rice available. The South-

---

[10] The pliability of the Siamese is well described by Philippe Mullender in "L'evolution récente de la Thailande," *Politique Etrangère,* XV (1950), 213-223.

Bevin on August 20, 1945, acknowledged the assistance received from the Siamese resistance movement and noted the Siamese denunciation of the declaration of war. *Parliamentary Debates,* House of Commons, Vol. 413, clmn. 299; Mr. McNeil's statement, Dec. 20, 1945, *Ibid.,* Vol. 417, clmns. 1700-1701.

[11] The text in the *New York Times,* Jan. 2, 1946. Siamese action may have been caused by an overestimation of Britain's imperialist interest. As the *Manchester Guardian,* January 2, 1946, put it: "She is as free as before, she has not become a protectorate, as she might have done in our more graceless

east Asia Command and later the Commissioner for Southeast Asia were concerned with the distribution of rice in the area. Through 1946 and 1947 monthly meetings were held to plan the distribution of rice. The allocations were initially determined by the International Emergency Food Council of the Food and Agricultural Organization of the United Nations. To supply food to this area Article XIV of the Siamese Peace Treaty bound the Siamese Government to supply without payment as much as one and a half million tons of surplus rice. This mildly punitive measure, based on the belief that huge stocks of rice had accumulated during the last years of the War, and that the food shortage had been intensified by Siamese collaboration with the Japanese, failed. In spite of this belief,[12] the urgency of the food situation in Asia caused the British government (May 3, 1946) to waive Article XIV and to agree to buy 1,200,000 tons of rise at £12 per ton with additional premiums for speedy delivery. But Siamese farmers preferred the higher price of a free market, and, subsequently, the quota was again reduced and the price raised.

2. *End of Empire in India, Ceylon and Burma.*

The aspirations of Indian nationalists for complete control of their affairs swelled to an irresistible demand during the War. On Aug. 8, 1942, the Indian Congress Party passed

---

days." See Alec Peterson, "Britain and Siam: The Latest Phase," *Pacific Affairs,* December, 1946. The following diverse estimates of the agreement may be amusing: "No former enemy ever fared so well." *Christian Science Monitor,* Jan. 4, 1946 "Siam gets off with her honor and her possessions in fair condition." *New York Times,* Jan. 3, 1946. "The agreement also creates for the British a special position in Siam, which is harmful to American trade and wholly unjustified in an independent country." *New York Herald Tribune,* Jan. 3, 1946.

[12] Sir Ben Smith, May 15, 1946, *Weekly Hansard,* House of Commons, No. 16, clmn. 1874. *The Times,* May 4, 1946.

a resolution demanding that the British "Quit India." Sir Stafford Cripps' offer of complete Indian self-government at the end of the War was rejected and British control over India during the remainder of the War was a major achievement of British imperial skill. The Viceroy, Lord Wavell, profited from the Hindu-Moslem division, but he was unable to secure adequate Indian participation in his government. The British Labour Government's promise of self-government was received with deep suspicion and was followed by ominous stirring throughout the country.

The great wrong of British imperialism has been not economic exploitation but the creation of an irresponsible temper among the victims of imperialism who are led to blame all their woes on British rule. The necessary decisions of any moment are therefore subordinated to the demand for the liquidation of imperial rule. Suspicion, often feeding on itself, negates any constructive proposal and any consideration of difficulties.

Nowhere is this irresponsible blindness more apparent than in the relations of the Congress Party to the Moslem League. The Congress Party tended to ignore the Moslem League or to deride it as a British separatist device. Earlier British offers to India had made the precondition that there should be general agreement on the settlement, which should also provide adequately for the protection of minority groups. This characteristic British emphasis has frequently caused them to be charged with divisive tactics. This unfair accusation, for the divisions of India were very real, may, however, be supported by the fact that the British often failed to act decisively for the mitigation of communal tensions and mistrust.

At any rate, on March 15, 1946, Prime Minister Attlee announced that it was for the Indians themselves to choose their future status and constitution. This decision, which was implemented by sending a Cabinet mission to India, took the lid off of the communal divisions of India. Riots, mutinies, and the initial unwillingness of Indian politicians to shoulder responsibility, drove Britain to a further step. The alternatives, as Sir Stafford Cripps pointed out on March 5, 1947, were to strengthen interim British control by increasing British personnel and troops in India or to make a further attempt to secure Indian agreement, supported by a warning that there was only a limited time during which Britain would maintain administrative responsibility for India. As the first course was unacceptable to the British and Indians, the British Government announced that it would withdraw from India in June, 1948. The prospect of independence had further undermined British power, and Britain, as Attlee put it, was determined to avoid the danger of having full responsibility without power.[13]

Within a week of his arrival in India (March 21, 1947), the new Viceroy, Lord Mountbatten, came to the conclusion "that a decision had to be taken at the earliest possible moment unless there was to be the risk of a general conflagration throughout the whole sub-continent."[14] The date for the transfer of sovereignty to the Indians was changed to Aug. 15, 1947. This decision worked wonders in convincing the Indians of British sincerity. Thereafter, Mountbatten's patience and tact were devoted to winning Indian agreement on some kind of settlement. The result was the creation of two new states. One of these, the Republic of

---

[13] Attlee, *Weekly Hansard,* House of Commons, No. 9, March 15, 1946, clmns. 1420-1426; Cripps, *Ibid.,* House of Commons, No. 44, March 5, 1947, clmns. 503-512; Attlee, *Ibid.,* House of Commons, No. 42, Feb. 20, 1947, clmns. 1405-1406.

[14] Quoted in Andrew Mellor, *India Since Partition* (New York, 1951), p. 22.

India, eventually associated itself with the British Common-wealth. The other, Pakistan, inherited a vulnerable economy, divided domains, a difficult defense position and all the tortuous difficulties of the Northwest frontier. This Moslem state became a full member of the Commonwealth. The successful and ingenious British efforts to have India associated with the Commonwealth caused Pakistan to resent apparent British favoritism to India, the larger state.[15] This irritation was peculiarly strong when Britain failed to support Pakistan's claim to Kashmir. The dispute over this area, claimed by India and Pakistan, nullified the military resources of the two states in a checkmate.

Lord Macaulay had said that the day on which India claimed independence, would be the proud fulfillment of British rule. The British had risen to the occasion. They had made their peace with Indian nationalism. Partition had been accompanied by communal massacres on a scale which no imperialist atrocity of the past could match even though the leaders and servants of the new states struggled manfully to cope with these horrors unleashed by the passing of the *Pax Britannica*.

This imperialist renunciation had its imponderable effect. It also greatly transformed the British imperial defense system. Britain lost the Indian army and bases which had helped to shelter the Middle East.[16]

Ceylon, too, refused to accept anything less than inde-

---

[15] Richard Symonds, *The Making of Pakistan* (London, 1950), pp. 168-173. General Smuts opposed the linking of the Indian Republic to the Commonwealth. "Great care should be used not to empty the Commonwealth concept. . . . The clear concept of the Commonwealth should be left intact and not be merged in vague relationships." *The Times,* April 11, 1949.

[16] The Iraki Premier, Nuri-es-Said Pasha, has insisted that Britain's abandonment of India makes obsolete the British effort to maintain bases in Iraq.

pendence, although she did make bases available to Britain. In January, 1948, Ceylon acquired Dominion status in the British Commonwealth.

Impoverished and unstable Burma, also, was not pleased with the slower progress towards self-government which the British Government proposed. By March 31, 1946, civilian rule was wholly restored, but the largest Burmese party, the Anti-Fascist People's Freedom League, refused to serve in the government. Indeed, unless tutelage involved very clear advantages, it is difficult to see how any nationalist party could settle for less than the offer to India. As the British Government had good grounds to fear an armed uprising, Prime Minister Attlee on December 20, 1946, stated that "the Burmese people should attain their self-government by the quickest and most convenient path possible," for Britain does "not desire to retain within the Commonwealth and Empire any unwilling peoples."[17] Here was capitulation out of weakness, for the very disorder of Burma and the necessity of a strong government, which the British could not provide, compelled the decision in favor of Burmese independence. The new status, complete independence established on January 4, 1948, wrought no miracle, and Burma under dedicated Socialists lapsed into civil war and further economic decay.[18]

3. *The Middle East.*

In this area vital for British defense, communications, investments and oil resources, Britain followed less successfully the policy of aligning herself with the forces of Asian

---

[17] *Weekly Hansard,* House of Commons, No. 37, Dec. 20, 1946, clmn. 2344.

[18] See "Burma Since the War," *The World Today,* IV (October, 1948), 437-446.

and Arab nationalism. Such a policy involved considerable difficulties, for British strategic interests and Arab nationalist demands did not necessarily coincide. Further, the policy raised the difficulties of an equitable and peaceful solution in Palestine to the nearly impossible.

In supporting the Arab League, Foreign Secretary Bevin was following the policy of the wartime Coalition Cabinet. The wartime and locally unpopular Middle East Supply Center and the almost viceregal office of Minister Resident were discontinued.[19] In their place was established the Middle East Office, not a joint Anglo-American enterprise, but an exclusively British affair. This Office, working under a committee in London, was established in Cairo to furnish to the Middle Eastern states upon request, commercial and technical information as well as technicians and experts. The hopes which inspired this office were expressed by *The Economist* in the following terms: "On the whole they [the British] have taught how to tax and police and administer justice, but not how to be literate or to kill flies. They are now ready in their own as well as Arab interests, to offer such teaching on an advisory basis in an effort to adjust the present glaring inequalities between rich and poor, and so to produce contentment and tranquility in the area."[20]

This objective, designed to render the legacy of imperialism more benevolent, was not effectively implemented, partly because of Arab mistrust which often became irresponsibility, partly because the British desire for an immediate accord meant support of existing conservative Arab gov-

[19] Prime Minister Attlee indicated his decision against the posts of Minister Resident on August 12, 1945. *The Times,* August 13, 1945.

[20] *The Economist,* CXLIX (December 1, 1945), 787. A writer in *Le Monde,* April 4, 1946, put the case more sharply. British imperial politics, he said, were in the course of reconstruction, for Britain in the Middle East had reached the very end of the era of promises.

ernments,[21] thereby diminishing the possibility of social reform and long-term stabilization, and partly because of the weakened economic position of Britain.

British policy was defined in general outlines during September, 1945, when Bevin began a series of meetings with British Middle Eastern diplomats and continued them into the difficult days of the London meeting of the Council of Foreign Ministers when the Soviet Union was manifesting a lively interest in the Mediterranean. On Sept. 20, 1945, a Foreign Office statement noted that Bevin and the British diplomats had examined "in all their aspects" the problems "presented in the Middle East by the imminent return to postwar conditions." Britain's policy would involve "strengthening the relations with the countries in the Middle East on the basis of mutual cooperation, and the promotion of their social and economic well-being."[22]

Bevin developed this theme in a speech to the Anglo-Egyptian Chamber of Commerce, where Egyptian nationalists were more urbane than in Cairo. The Foreign Secretary, equally amiable, told the Chamber that the tree of security was not yet full grown, that Britain did not want to dominate Egypt and that in such a vital area, with security still but a tender sapling, there was need of mutual defense. Thus he would "like to see a great defence built up, not on the basis of Great Britain protecting Egypt, but of

---

[21] Bevin's speech (May 24, 1946) presented a penetrating analysis of the anti-imperialist temper of Egypt. "Do not forget that any country which has been occupied by another's forces has an inferiority complex. . . . Our relations with Egypt, unfortunately, rest on a very narrow basis. We have never gained the gratitude and thankfulness of the masses of the people in Egypt. We have added, as a result of our connection with Egypt, very great wealth to the country, but it has never flowed down to the fellaheen. The result is that it has been an extremely narrow circle with whom we have dealt." *Weekly Hansard,* House of Commons, No. 18, clmns. 787, 789.

[22] *The Times,* Sept. 21, 1945.

the two nations on a basis of partnership between the Middle East and ourselves."[23] This simply posed again the previously insoluble problem of transforming privileges, once secured by domination, into privileges granted by the "injured equal." In the Treaty of 1936 Egypt had agreed to grant such privileges only because of her fear of Italian agression.

As a model of Britain's future relations with the Arab world, the Emir Abdullah of Trans-Jordan, whose army was trained and supported by Britain, was informed on January 18, 1946, that His Majesty's Government was prepared to recognize Trans-Jordan as a sovereign state. There, the British could look for bases and a seaport, Akqaba, giving access to the Red Sea.

In two other areas, however, the British approach ran into difficulties. The disposition of the Italian colony, Libya, was complicated by a characteristic fragmentation of the problem.[24] Britain had promised the Senussi of Cyrenaica that their land would not be restored to Italian rule. The Soviet Union asked for the trusteeship of a part of Libya, Tripolitania. France was opposed to Libyan independence, and the Arab League was hostile to an Italian or British trusteeship. As this issue was not settled by the Foreign

---

[23] *The Times,* Nov. 2, 1945. The problem was more frankly expressed in the Royal Empire Society Address of Lord Altrincham, who, as Sir Edward Grigg, had been Minister Resident in the Middle East in 1944-1945. He recognized that the remnants of tutelage had to go and had to be succeeded by equal and mutually beneficent partnership, and that spheres of influence had also been outmoded. But, he added, nations have special interests in certain regions: Britain in the Middle East and Russia in her immediate neighbors. *The Times,* November 15, 1945.

[24] In view of Churchill's acceptance of the demand for Germany's unconditional surrender, Britain's wartime eagerness to prevent the disintegration of the Italian administrative machinery in Italian East Africa makes a striking contrast. Lord Rennell of Rodd, *British Military Administration of Occupied Territories in Africa, During the Years 1941-1947* (London, 1948), pp. 102‑103.

Ministers, it was eventually referred to the General Assembly of the United Nations.

An attempt to deal with Syria and Lebanon also came under United Nations' and Arab fire. On December 13, 1945, Britain and France announced that they planned immediate conversations about a simultaneous evacuation of their forces in Syria and Lebanon, contingent on "the organization of collective security" there.[25] Syria and Lebanon protested that they had not been consulted. When further conversations stalled in further disagreement, the case was presented to the Security Council on February 5, 1946, where the complaint received the warm support of the Soviet Union. The British and French positions in Syria and Lebanon were vulnerable, and, in spite of a Soviet veto of a conciliatory resolution, British and French troops were withdrawn, and France was defeated in the Levant. This was not greatly regretted by the British, who saw in the ejection of France the opportunity for a greater cohesion of the Arab states.

4. *Egypt*.

In Anglo-Egyptian relations, strategic interest in the defense of the Suez Canal, direfully complicated by Palestine, was the fundamental British consideration, although Britain was prepared to be ingenious in meeting the demands of Egyptian nationalism. Defense of the Canal area was the chief strategic interest, not so much to insure the use of the Canal in wartime as to deny the use of the area to any hostile power. The Wafd Party, placed in office by British action in 1942, was dismissed from office by King Farouk in Octo-

---

[25] Text reprinted in the *Chronology of International Events and Documents*, II (December 20, 1945-January 6, 1946), 30.

ber, 1944, immediately after its leader, Nahas Pasha, had successfully prepared the ground for the Arab League. His successor, Ahmed Mahir Pasha, was assassinated four months after he had declared war on the Axis. The next premier, Nokrashy Pasha, was ultimately driven to ask Britain to revise the Anglo-Egyptian Treaty of 1936, which provided for mutual assistance in time of war and allowed Britain to garrison the Canal Zone.

Egypt had become a British military base in the course of the War. This occupation of the country confirmed nationalist suspicions that Britain's recognition of Egyptian sovereignty was in effect nullified by the British interpretation of the Treaty of 1936. This suspicion placed a heavy burden upon the sufficiently difficult effort to seek a mutually satisfactory solution. Another complication was the fact that the Wafd Party, the traditionally nationalist party, Egypt's only party with a large popular following and adequate party organization, was at odds with King Farouk and out of office. It was all but inevitable that the Wafd should seek political advantage by attacking any diplomatic negotiations as a sell-out of the national cause.

The nationalist demands began to be made long before the War ended, and it is surprising that Bevin made no conciliatory gesture[26] in 1945, although he could plead that in spite of many public demands by Egyptian officials, none

---

[26] Such as an immediate evacuation of British troops out of the major Egyptian cities. This was the burden of the Conservative attack on the later concessions of the Labour Government. This approach is based on the belief that a gesture can satisfy a nationalist demand. The basic weakness of the British bargaining position was described by Lord Lloyd nearly twenty-five years ago: "If the abortive Sarwat treaty negotiations showed anything it was the difficulty at this date, when we have already given Egypt so much, of finding sufficient further concessions to make it worth her while to accept our minimum desiderata and thus to liquidate 1922." Sir Charles Petrie, *The Life and Letters of the Right Hon. Sir Austen Chamberlain* (London, 1940), II, p. 358.

was presented to him until December, 1945. Such a claim, however, was disingenuous, for the Egyptian demand was delayed on the request of the British Embassy in Cairo. Under the terms of the Treaty, revision could be made after ten years, and the Egyptian request called for negotiations which would include the position of the Sudan, nominally ruled jointly by Britain and Egypt but in effect by the British Government through the Foreign Office. After a month's delay the British replied coldly, and indicated that recent experience had confirmed the soundness of the 1936 Treaty. This was followed by the inevitable Egyptian cabinet crisis. Sidky Pasha, the new Premier, appointed a delegation to negotiate revision of the Treaty, and the Wafd, upon being refused new elections and control of the delegation, stirred up an opposition, riots and strikes of students and workers, which made agreement impossible. A British delegation was approved and a new approach was "reluctantly" agreed upon.[27] The British government, to prove its good will and to assure the Egyptians of their equality, proposed to evacuate all their forces from Egypt. Negotiations were to determine the schedule of evacuation, and to provide for the mutual defense of the strategic areas.

The effective Conservative challenge to this policy in the House of Commons reveals the calculations of the British Government. At the moment, the British expected to remain in Palestine, although for a brief period there was some thought of abandoning major bases in the Mediterranean for a major base in Kenya.[28] Churchill argued that if the British were to use Palestine as a base, they would encounter trouble there and impair the possibility of Ameri-

---

[27] Herbert Morrison in *Weekly Hansard,* House of Commons, No. 15, May 7, 1946, clmn. 903.

[28] Elizabeth Monroe, "British Interests in the Middle East," *The Middle East Journal,* II (April, 1948), 130-131.

can cooperation with Britain. He, also, discounted the value of Cyrenaica and any expectations of Egyptian gratitude.[29] Fundamentally, Churchill insisted, a treaty of alliance would be of no value if Britain was not permitted to maintain troops at strategic positions. To begin the removal of troops as a preliminary to negotiations was "tantalizing diplomacy," for "in fact we concede the whole point at issue, subject to conditions which cannot be obtained."[30]

The offer appears to have been made to save Egyptian face. The limits of the Labour Government's gesture appeared in Attlee's reply to hostile questions. If the British Government was not satisfied with the negotiations, the 1936 Treaty would continue. But, apart from its Treaty rights, the British Government thought that it had a trump card in the Sudan. Indeed, as events showed, the British had no appreciation of the strength of Egyptian feeling about "the unity of the Nile Valley,"[31] a slogan which made impossible Egyptian acceptance of the British position that the Sudanese should eventually be allowed freely to choose between independence and association with Egypt. British administration in the Sudan appeared as a model of beneficent imperialism. Egyptian control, to put the very minimum case, would not be an improvement. By promoting Su-

---

[29] This is a curious argument on Churchill's part, for he has long argued that Egypt in gratitude for British protection during the War should greatly reduce her sterling claims on Britain.

[30] *Weekly Hansard*, House of Commons, No. 18, May 24, 1946, clmns. 770-783.

[31] Simply stated the British were surprised to learn that their Sudan was claimed by the Egyptians, and the Egyptians shared the same sentiments. Mr. Churchill's earlier account (1899) of the Sudan readily explains the Egyptian demand. "The grasp of England upon Egypt has been strengthened twofold by the events of the war [which gained the Sudan]. The joint action and ownership of the two countries in the basin of the Upper Nile form an additional bond between them. The command of the vital river is an irresistible weapon." *The River War* (London, 1951), p. 364.

danese self-government, Britain could attempt to brand Egypt as the imperialist state, and make certain the breakdown of the treaty discussions, if Egypt continued her refusal to make any serious concessions.[32]

The course of negotiations was not made smoother by frequent Egyptian "leaks" to the press. On one occasion, some Egyptians characteristically described proposed arrangements for mutual defense as more onerous than foreign occupation.[33] To break the stalemate Sidky Pasha himself came to London on October 17, 1946. His departure on a peace mission from riot-bound Cairo was marred only by a threat to bomb his plane.

Egyptian statesmen have often been more moderate in London than they are at home. At any rate, Bevin and Sidky initialled a draft agreement which with wonderful obfuscation saved everybody's face and destroyed itself. They agreed that the Sudanese "within the framework of the unity between the Sudan and Egypt under the common crown of Egypt" would eventually be allowed to exercise "the right to choose the future status of the Sudan." Pending fulfillment, the British were to continue present control.[34]

---

[32] The process of preparing Sudanese participation in government was notably accelerated during 1946. This was part of British diplomacy, for the Sudan was administered through the Foreign Office. A typical, moderate Egyptian view was expressed by Senator L. A. Fanous, who said that Sudanese nationality was a laughing matter and warned the British against creating an African Alsace-Lorraine. *Manchester Guardian,* Oct. 31, 1946.

[33] *New York Times,* May 23, 1946. British press comments usually regretted that Egypt thought only in nationalist terms, whereas the British entreated her to think in regional terms. The Egyptian reply was twofold: (1) partnership with the British would involve them in foreign conflict; (2) regional defense arrangements were unnecessary in the era of the U.N.

[34] The strictures of Jon Kimche in *Seven Fallen Pillars* (London, 1950), pp. 61-75, are fair enough. "The Bevin-Sidky formula . . . was so subtle as to be meaningless. But no one has yet (as far as is known) suggested a better one." *The Spectator,* CLXXXVI (April 13, 1951), 478.

On his return Sidky recalled that he had promised to bring the Sudan back to Egypt and affirmed his success.[35] This brought forth the explanation from Britain that the condominium in the Sudan had merely been affirmed, along with a promise that the Sudan should be free to choose its future status. In spite of the protests of the Egyptian Treaty delegation, the Government against growing violence took steps to conclude the treaty. This difficult situation was inflamed by a statement of the Governor General of the Sudan, who emphasized that nothing would be permitted to deflect the Sudanese (British) authorities from preparing for self-government and free determination of the Sudanese future.[36]

When Sidky resigned, his successor, Nokrashy Pasha, a moderate man, announced: "When I say unity of the Sudan and Egypt under the Egyptian Crown, I mean permanent unity."

The face-saving gesture was valuable only if successful. If it failed to produce an agreement, the gesture would appear as hollow insincerity, compounding suspicion and mistrust. Later negotiations were to be all the more difficult.[37] After February, 1947, British forces were expected to leave Palestine. Meanwhile, Britain was all the more determined to maintain its position in the Canal Zone, for there was new hope of defending the Eastern Mediterranean when after the declaration of the Truman Doctrine,

---

[35] *The Observer*, Oct. 27, 1946.

[36] *Manchester Guardian*, December 9, 1946. It is difficult not to see in this a deliberate attempt to destroy the possibility of an agreement. An Egyptian quoted in *La Bourse Egyptienne*, January 9, 1947, observed that Britain in the face of Soviet expansion was resolved to keep Egypt as a sphere of influence. Sidky Pasha in statements to the Arab press innocently indicated that he never understood what had happened. Initially he blamed British imperialism but he later argued that the draft treaty, afforded gains to Egypt. *Manchester Guardian*, January 3, 1947; *The Times*, February 10, 1947.

the United States took over the support of Turkey and Greece. In the summer of 1947 Egypt finally appealed to the Security Council, arguing that the Anglo-Egyptian Treaty was invalid and demanding the evacuation of British troops from Egypt and the Sudan. Nokrashy Pasha's legalistic arguments were unsuccessful, and at home his efforts were scored for their treacherous moderation.[38] Thus, in Egypt an initial effort to reduce commitments was transformed into an attempt to make face-saving adjustments while maintaining bases necessary for imperial defense.

5. *Iran*.

Soviet pressure on the Middle East took many forms, including a bid for an Italian Colony and demands for concessions in the Turkish Straits. Britain's Egyptian experience suggests that the most promising course would have been support of Middle Eastern nationalism. In Iran, however, the Soviet Union initially attempted to take parts of the country under its control. This action was made possible by the presence of Soviet troops in Iran as a result of the joint wartime occupation of the country by Britain and Russia. To the Iranians this was an unhappily needless reminder that Iranian independence was primarily supported by the mutual hostility of Russia and Britain. Moments of accord in 1907 and 1941 had resulted in the strangling of Persia.

At the end of the War British interests in Iran included banking, the Anglo-Iranian oil fields and refinery and the necessity of keeping a strong foreign power from dominat-

---

[37] Gibb, "Anglo-Egyptian Relations. A Revaluation," *International Affairs* (Sept., 1951).

[38] Herbert W. Briggs, "Rebus Sic Stantibus Before the Security Council: The Anglo-Egyptian Question," *The American Journal of International Law*, XLIII (Oct., 1949), 762-769.

ing Iran and menacing the Persian Gulf and Indian Ocean. Britain wanted an independent Iran as a future buffer against the Soviet Union.[39]

The able British diplomatic representative in Iran from 1939 to 1946, Sir Reader Bullard, has said that "the existence of a strong Iran is essential to British interests."[40] Late in 1945, however, it appeared that under the cover of the Soviet occupation Iran was being dismembered. In the Soviet sphere, Azerbaijan set up a Communist government and cut itself off from the Iranian government. The British Government protested. At the Moscow Conference, December, 1945, Bevin proposed an Anglo-American-Russian Commission to consider various Iranian problems. The suggestion was rejected by the Russians. To the Iranians it looked as though the British Government was considering the possibility of a spheres-of-influence deal. Initially Bevin did not favor Iran's appeal to the Security Council, about the Soviet infringement of Iranian sovereignty, but he did support the complaint when it was made. Moreover, although the Soviet troops delayed their departure, Russian expansionist policy was for the moment defeated. The Communist sponsored states in Iran were eventually overthrown and in 1947 the Majlis, the Persian Parliament, rejected an oil

---

[39] A newspaper which voiced the opinions of the Iranian political leader, Seyyid Zia ed-Din, contained the following in its issue of Jan. 16, 1945: "If our nation is resolved to resist illegal Soviet influence and its interference in internal affairs, Great Britain will certainly be faithful to her pledges and will defend Iran's independence. If, however, we shall cede without resistance before force, then Great Britain will also try to secure some gains for herself at the expense of Iran. If we allow our northern provinces to be overpowered by Communism Great Britain will take over our southern provinces, and then Iran will be partitioned." Quoted in George Lenczowski, *Russia and the West in Iran, 1918-1948* (Ithaca, 1949), p. 245.

[40] Sir Reader Bullard, *Britain and the Middle East* (London, 1951), p. 143.

agreement with Russia, presumably the price demanded for the evacuation of Soviet troops. The sinuous politics of Premier Qhavam won a momentary triumph, in spite of the fact that Persian military strength was negligible.

In the course of winning the victory over Soviet influence, there were a number of risings in Southern Iran against the prominence in Qhavam's Government of the Communist-dominated Tudeh Party.[41] In July and August of 1946 the Communists inspired a great strike in the Anglo-Iranian oil fields. The British Labour Government, for the last time in the Middle East, riposted with the policy of sending troops and ships from India to Basra in Iraq where the British have treaty rights. This strong show was accompanied by a statement that the objective of the troops was to be ready to defend British interest in nearby southern Persia. Also, in traditional fashion, it was presently announced by the Foreign Office that the new troops were merely replacements; and, to complete the old melodrama, there were the statements of the Iranian Prime Minister that Iran was perfectly capable of managing its own affairs, and the final British position, that Britain, of course, recognized the Iranian Government's responsibility.[42]

Iranian rejection of the Soviet oil treaty was strongly supported by the United States. The Soviet defeat, however, made possible a new line of Soviet attack. Only Britain remained as a major foreign concessionaire in Iran. Freed by defeat the Soviet tactics could now revert to the support of Iranian nationalism against the British oil company.

---

[41] George Lenczowski, *op. cit.*, pp. 304-306, believes that the British inspired these tribal risings. Sir Reader Bullard, *op. cit.*, p. 143, states emphatically that the British Government "had decided in 1941 that on no account was any encouragement to be given to any Iranian tribe against its Government, and they had applied that policy strictly ever since."

[42] *Chronology of International Events and Documents*, II (July 8-July

6. *Palestine.*

The projected cooperation with the Arab world was terribly threatened by the problem of the twice promised land, Palestine. After the Nazi massacres, most of the remnants of European Jewry were determined to go to Palestine. The Zionists, who simply ignored the claims of the Palestine Arabs and disregarded the feelings of the Arab states, were determined to build a Jewish State in Palestine. The Arabs refused to consider a Jewish state and offered the Jews only the prospect of being a tolerated minority in an Arab state. A solution of this conflict clearly required mediation backed by the threat of force.

Britain as the mandatory power was initially responsible for the provision of force. Forthright mediation, however, involved grave difficulties. First of all, the Labour Party had many times rejected the British White Paper (1939), which had drastically limited Jewish immigration to Palestine. The program of the Labour Party favored Zionist aspirations. On the other hand, Labour's Foreign Secretary, Mr. Bevin, accepted the policy of supporting the Arab League. This, in turn, was certain to cause difficulties with the United States, where important segments of public opinion were favorable to the Zionist cause. Widespread and widely supported Jewish terrorism intensified Britain's difficulties.

Bevin found the thorniness of the problem very perplexing, and, like many other Labour Ministers, he soon came to believe that, in its earlier stand on Palestine, the Labour

---

21, 1946), 419, *ibid.,* II (July 22-August 11, 1946), 447, 451-452. The newspaper accounts of this incident, apart from the Russian press, are very scanty. A particularly entrancing event in the midst of this turmoil was a mass demonstration of the Tudeh Party in Teheran against the Franco Government. (July 21, 1946).

Party had been deceived by Zionist spokesmen, who simply dismissed the reality of Arab feelings. Nothing reveals more strikingly the shallow irresponsibility of Labour's thinking on foreign affairs than Bevin's abandonment of Labour's position on Palestine. Nonetheless, Bevin actually staked his future on the solution of the Palestine question.[43] His proposed solution, an Anglo-American Committee of Inquiry, was composed of the conventional policy of delaying a decision and of a bold attempt to associate the United States with that decision. Speaking at a press conference on November 13, 1945, Bevin emphasized that Palestine was only part of a far wider issue which interested the Arab world throughout the Middle East. The Foreign Secretary further expressed his regret that the Balfour Declaration had been unilateral and had taken no account of the Arabs, who, and here he became unrealistic, were disposed to be generous, if they alone were not asked to bear the burden of the Jewish problem. He looked for no difficulty on that point, because the British Government was committed not to a Jewish state but to a Jewish National Home. The new committee was asked to look into the whole problem of Jewish refugees in Europe, and the Foreign Secretary expressed the hope that the Jews would not abandon Europe.[44]

The Anglo-American Committee's report, which envisioned Britain's continuation in Palestine, was stillborn.

---

[43] Jon Kimche, *Seven Fallen Pillars* (London, 1950), pp. 141-143.

[44] *The Times,* November 14, 1945. Bevin's acute embarrassment about Palestine was bluntly expressed during a debate on the United Nations Charter. A Labour M.P., George Griffiths, attacked the Conservative M.P., Colonel Stanley, who said that his party had been wise enough to be silent about Palestine. Griffiths retorted that the Conservatives had been sitting on the fence, and Stanley submitted that such a course was better than coming down prematurely on the wrong side. Bevin then interjected: "You cannot always get off [the fence]." *Parliamentary Debates,* House of Commons, Vol. 413, Aug. 23, 1945, clmns. 934-935.

President Truman approved a part of the Commission's report, which urged that 100,000 Jews be admitted to Palestine. The United States Government, however, was not prepared to send forces to join the British in imposing the solution. Subsequent plans came to nothing, for the British Government took the impossible position that a solution would have to be acceptable to both sides. It would not use force to maintain a solution.

The Jews, desperately abandoning Europe and ardently ready for the labor of creating a new nation, in typical colonial fashion derided Arab opposition as a British legend. The Arabs, equally unyielding and irresponsible, argued that the withdrawal of British forces would end the pretensions of the Jews. Britain, seeking Arab friendship and hoping to depend upon Arab military resources for the defense of the Middle East, was not prepared to use force against the Arabs, and as the United States took an opposite line, the British determined to surrender the mandate to the United Nations.

The surrender, however, was made on terms that made war inevitable. The British Government would not enforce a United Nations' solution and would not admit United Nations' administrative personnel into Palestine while British forces remained there.[45] Although American policy was no more moderate or responsible, the British position was based on an amazing military miscalculation. Mr. Bevin's

---

[45] R. M. Graves, a British subject and the last mayor of Jerusalem under the Mandate, wrote in his diary the following comment on the decision to terminate the Mandate and withdraw the British troops: "It is difficult to take this declaration seriously. If it is meant seriously, I can't comment without profanity." A later entry noted that on the Palestine question reason would not move Bevin who "is cemented up to the knees and can't be moved." Graves, *Experiment in Anarchy* (London, 1949), pp. 88-94. G. L. Arnold sees in Britain's failure in Palestine the result of the decline of Liberal imperialism, the imperialism of progress. "Lessons of Palestine," *Nineteenth Century and After*, CXLIV (October, 1948), 192-201.

government expected the Arabs to win.

The defeat of the Arab states was followed by some exceedingly clumsy British maneuvres in Trans-Jordan, still under strong British control. The spectacle of Jordan asking for British military assistance in case of an Israeli attack was very similar to the British Foreign Office talking to itself. British planes, cooperating with the Egyptians, flew over the battle lines and were shot down by the Israelis (Jan. 7, 1949). For a final muddlement, the British Government warned Israel that the fighting in the Negev area might cause Britain to intervene under the terms of the British treaties with Egypt and Trans-Jordan. This was supreme folly, for the Egyptian Government did not desire the humiliation of being saved by Britain.[46]

The British Government finally desisted from this course and recognized Israel in April, 1950. Thereafter, British relations with Israel became fairly cordial. In the Arab states the aftermath of defeat was not followed by sober self-examination. They had not been realistic about the war. Their peoples had not been informed of the military disasters. Over 700,000 Arabs were refugees from Palestine. An intransigent temper towards Israel as the enemy and toward Britain as the scapegoat made a settlement in the Middle East appear as difficult as, earlier, the solution of the Palestine problem had been.

7. *Greece and Turkey.*

The turmoil of the Middle East and Asia was matched by the difficulties which Britain confronted in Greece and Turkey. Control of the Mediterranean transit area was important in British plans for the defense of the Middle East.

---

[46] *The Observer,* Jan. 9 and 16, 1949.

Greece and Turkey were vital positions which the British sought to keep out of the hands of any potential enemy. During the War Britain was allied with Turkey, and supported the Greek Government-in-exile and the Greek resistance movement.

After British troops landed in Greece in October, 1944, they were faced by a Communist *coup* in December. The attempted *coup* ended any pretense of cooperation between the leftist resistance groups and the Greek Government. British mediation in the subsequent civil war resulted in the Varkiza agreement (Feb. 12, 1945) which temporarily stopped the fighting and promised a plebiscite to determine whether Greece would be a monarchy or republic. The British Government sought to work through non-Communist Greek authorities and, as a result, had to rely on the rightists and monarchists.[47]

Subsequently, the British Government approved a decision to hold elections before the plebiscite. The left, especially the Communists, opposed and then boycotted the election of March 31, 1946, which resulted in a Royalist victory. A plebiscite (Oct. 1, 1946) called back King George II to the throne of Greece.

The events in Greece, like Franco's victory in Spain, produced a crisis in the liberal conscience of the world. The Soviet Union exploited this feeling by bringing a complaint to the Security Council about the presence of British troops in

---

[47] Mr. Bevin, later, expressed his excessively unsubtle attitude towards the Greek struggle. Addressing a Greek Parliamentary delegation, he said: "I have had a few disturbing moments since those days, what with Trade Union Congresses and Labour Parties and so on (and even my dearest friends sometimes have doubted my wisdom), but I have always stuck to one principle —and I am an old trade unionist—he who fights with me, I never desert. And it does not matter what happens, however wayward he might become." *Foreign Office Bulletin,* July 22, 1949.

Greece. Bevin's reply frankly associated his Greek policy with Churchill's.[48] He branded the Soviet action as a diversion, and rightly noted the economic cost of British assistance to Greece,[49] which from October, 1944, to May, 1947, amounted to £132,000,000.[50] During 1946 the British Government found itself unable to meet the mounting financial needs of Greece. Serious guerilla warfare began against the Greek Government in the autumn of 1946. Early in 1947 the British Government informed the United States that Britain could no longer support the Greek Government adequately.

British contributions to Turkey's defense also came to an end at that time. During the years, 1938-1947, British aid to Turkey had amounted to more than £90,000,000. During the War Turkish forces had been mobilized to protect the country's neutrality.[51] Before the end of the War the Soviet Union had told Turkey that it would not renew the Treaty of Friendship between the two countries unless considerable changes were made. These included the revision of the Montreux Convention concerning the Turkish Straits. The Soviet Union insisted that the Straits be controlled by the Black Sea states and that they be closed to the warships of all other states. The Soviet Union also demanded bases in the

---

[48] "Have I or my Government, or the previous Government under Mr. Churchill (because we are all in it) in going to the aid of Greece" etc. *United Nations Security Council Official Records,* I (First series, No. 1, Jan. 17-Feb. 16, 1946), p. 88.

[49] Bevin's defense of British policy had no remarkable success. *The Manchester Guardian,* Feb. 16, 1946, commented: "It is profoundly disquieting to an Englishman to find that the British Empire . . . should appear increasingly as a vaster and more sympathetic ramshackle empire on the Habsburg model."

[50] "The Troubled Outlook in Greece," *The World Today,* IV (1948), 465.

[51] J. Daniel, "Turkey's Position in the Post-War World," *The Year Book of World Affairs, 1951* (London, 1951), p. 215.

Turkish Straits and the provinces of Kars and Ardahan. The United States and Britain were prepared for minor modifications of the Montreux Convention but they supported the Turkish rejection of these Soviet demands. The Turks supported their refusal by continuing the costly mobilization of their forces.

During 1946 the United States made a vigorous display of its naval power in the Mediterranean. American interest in the oil of the Middle East was increased by new concessions and purchasing arrangements with the Anglo-Iranian Oil Company. Finally, with Britain unable to maintain its commitments of support to Greece and Turkey, the United States stepped in with financial and military assistance to Greece and Turkey and a pledge of American assistance to countries struggling against Communist aggression. (March 12, 1947).

Britain, then, had reduced its commitments. Britain had tried to come to terms with Asiatic nationalism by granting sovereignty to most of its major Asiatic possessions. Britain failed to solve the riddle of the promises in Palestine, and had thereby embittered the Arab world with which the British Government sought partnership. Middle Eastern difficulties continued. Finally, financial weakness had compelled her to yield to the United States responsibility for Greece and Turkey, the unimposing bastions against the eruption of Soviet power into the Aegean and the Mediterranean.

CHAPTER FOUR

The Logic of Disagreement: Recovery And/or the Grand Alliance

"Should we draw closer to Europe—there is another question, an aim at creating under the Supreme World Council, a living union, an entity in Europe, a United States of Europe? Or, again, should we concentrate upon our own Imperial and Commonwealth organisation, upon our fraternal association with the United States, and put our trust in the English Channel in air power and in sea power?"

Churchill, 1944

1. *Turning Point: Marshall's Offer and Bevin's Initiative.*

The decisive year, 1947, opened, not with promise but lowering disaster. The heavy winter snows of 1946-47, accompanied by a coal shortage, further weakened Britain's position. Transportation was curtailed and industrial production stopped for a time and declined for a longer period. Food supplies throughout the world dwindled as drought prevailed in Southeast Asia and Europe's winter destroyed the spring crops. British commitments had been reduced but, even so, there was doubt that Britain could hold its position. The abandonment of Greece had become the occasion for the United States to proclaim unilaterally the Truman Doctrine of Containment. Where and how would the Soviet Union be contained? Vital positions on the Mediterranean were to be held. Britain, sheltered by American aid to Greece,

87

could be firmer in Egypt. But what strength was there in Europe, "a rubble heap, a charnelhouse, a breeding ground of pestilence and hate?"[1] Here and there was the appearance of a courageous action, as in France and Italy, where governments were formed without the Communist Party. But seriously challenged, how could this stand be maintained?

The insecurity, which this question expresses, arose less from the menace of Soviet power and propaganda than from the economic weakness of Western Europe. This weakness was spectacularly revealed in inadequate supplies of consumer goods and in an apparently chronic shortage of dollars. The insufficiency of consumer goods was responsible for the prevalence of the black market and a breakdown of goods exchanged between town and country. Contagion palsied inter-European trade, and international trade itself wound up in the unbalance of dollar payments.

Thus Europe was living on a dangerous margin. Coal was short everywhere and heavy snowfalls could actually halt the movement of British coal, the production of factories and even domestic heating. For want of a nail there might be general disaster. In March, 1947, the rations of Bizonal Germany were reduced, and, promptly, coal and industrial production shrivelled.

The first condition of European strength, then, was recovery. But recovery itself required the recovery of Germany. Germany, however, was truncated, and Soviet policy offered only the following alternatives: a Soviet promise to treat Germany as an economic unit on condition that the Soviet Union have a share in controlling the industrial Ruhr and that the German economy be overwhelmed by reparations payments to the Soviet Union; a divided Germany,

---

[1] Churchill, speech at United Europe meeting, *Europe Unite* (London, 1950), p. 78.

where a recovery effort could be made at the cost of abandoning any immediate hope of cooperating with the Soviet Union in Germany.

Bevin had warned the Soviet Union of the consequences of disagreement. In spite of the tempered optimism of his broadcast speech (Dec. 22, 1946), he had affirmed Britain's real position at the meeting of the Council of Foreign Ministers in New York (November, 1946). There, he had sought agreement on a code of conduct which would have mitigated Soviet use of the veto power. "We in Britain are now at the point where we must establish our general policy. We had hoped that the debates here would allow us to tell the British people that we are prepared to base our policy on the United Nations. Unfortunately, as things now stand, this will be impossible."[2]

The Moscow meeting of the Conference of Foreign Ministers (March-April, 1947) clearly indicated that the Soviet Union was not prepared for the negotiation of a peace treaty with Germany. Indeed, as Soviet interest was to promote instability, there was no serious inducement for Soviet cooperation. Six weeks of fruitless negotiation had been harrowing for Bevin. At the railway station, on his departure, Bevin ironically tried to teach Vyshinsky to sing "The more we are together."[3] On several later occasions, Bevin boasted of his monumental patience and expressed the belief that he must have been born again. In May his weary hope was "that by next November we [the Foreign Ministers] shall have said so much to one another that we shall

---

[2] *The Observer*, Nov. 24, 1946.

[3] Sir Maurice Peterson, *Both Sides of the Curtain* (London, 1950), p. 264. The British Ambassador did not consider this to be irony. "I approved the spirit of the performance but felt little disposed to applaud the sentiment. It went dead against the experience of the preceding weeks."

be tired of talking and will be ready to agree instead."[4]
What could Britain do? Bevin's reply excused his apparent
lack of initiative about European organization and recovery. "What did I have to organize it with? What could I
offer? I had neither coal, goods, nor credit, I was not in
the same position as my predecessors at the end of the Napoleonic Wars, who devised the policy, for nearly 20 years,
of spending our surplus exports to rehabilitate the world.
It was a case of our exports then. I did not have them. Therefore, I cannot be accused now of not taking a line to help
Western Europe. I have nothing with which to do it. I have
not had one ton of spare coal to ship to Western Europe to
help in rehabilitation. I have had nothing with which to
negotiate."[5]

This feeling of impotence explains the long continuation of the shadow play of Big Three cooperation. If the
very self-interests of the Four Powers in restraining Germany and in recovery did not produce cooperation, small
measures alone were possible, while the big problems loomed
in hypnotic largeness. The lesser states could do little, unless the United States faced the logic of disagreement and
was prepared to build up a bloc of powers to check Soviet
pressure.

This logic of disagreement was not inexorably followed

---

[4] *Report of the 46th Annual Conference of the Labour Party* (London,
1947), pp. 176, 182. Another comment on the Moscow Conference is revealing: "Only for the first week of the Conference was there any pretence that
the game was patience, that a solution creditable and satisfactory to all might
be reached. . . . So they switched to poker, but made little progress. No one's
hand was "seen" at Moscow, except perhaps that of M. Bidault, who was in
no position to conceal its weakness. For the rest the game is still on. It will
last another seven months at least, till the Foreign Ministers meet again in
London. By then, the players think, someone may have lost his nerve." *The
Round Table,* XXXVII (June, 1947), 225.

[5] *Weekly Hansard,* House of Commons, No. 57, June 19, 1947, clmn.
2354.

at once. The Marshall offer of American assistance to a joint European recovery effort did not exclude the Soviet Union. Bevin himself said that the plan would "throw a bridge to link east and west."[6] Molotov was invited by Bidault and Bevin to discuss the offer in Paris. In the Commons Bevin was very blunt. Not Britain and the United States but the Soviet Union had been dividing Europe. "The guiding principle that I shall follow in any talks will be speed. . . . I shall not be a party to holding up the economic recovery of Europe by the finesse of procedure, or terms of reference, or all the paraphernalia which may go with it. There is too much involved."[7]

In the Conference at Paris Bevin insisted on the necessity of a joint European effort, for that was the prerequisite of Marshall's offer. Molotov in behalf of the sovereignty of states argued that the countries should make known the catalogue of their individual needs. He warned Britain and France of the consequences of disagreement with the Soviet Union. Bevin replied; "My country has faced grave consequences and threats before, and it is not the sort of prospect which will deter us from doing what we consider to be our duty."[8] The meeting with Molotov ended. On July 3, Britain and France invited all European governments, except Russia and Spain, to meet in Paris on July 12 to initiate cooperative plans for European reconstruction. With Bevin following the principle of speed, a Committee of European Economic Cooperation was promptly

---

[6] Speech in London, June 13, 1947.

[7] Bevin identified the Soviet Union with the political persecution which the Labour Party had once fought. He remarked that the Party would not tolerate Communists in its own ranks. Britain might have to face the fact of a conflict of ideologies. "When people know that we understand what they are doing, they are less likely to do it next time." *Weekly Hansard,* House of Commons, No. 57, June 19, 1947, clmns. 2353-2356.

[8] July 2, 1947.

established. Technical committees were set to work and by September 22 a two-volume report of plans and requirements had been sent to Secretary of State Marshall. This planning had taken only two weeks more than the Moscow Conference.

Meanwhile, the British financial position had declined again. Britain in compliance with the American Loan Agreement gradually made sterling freely convertible with the dollar and on July 15, 1947, made it wholly so. The American Loan was drawn on for $1,300,000,000 in July and August. The unbalance of world trade and, particularly, the voracious world demand for dollars, rendered convertibility impossible. With only $400,000,000 of the credit remaining, the British government suspended convertibility, and was duly confirmed in its restrictionism.

2. *The Limits of Cooperation.*

With this reminder of weakness, Britain embarked upon a policy of European cooperation. This was no new Grand Alliance, but an effort to achieve strength through cooperative recovery. The contradictions in this objective were soon apparent. If Britain was to recover, she had to use her world interests to the full. This involved utilizing the resources of the Commonwealth, Empire and sterling area. The immediate stress in Britain was on her world and not her European position. In the work of recovery Britain was to insist on all the advantages of Imperial Preferences and all the opportunities offered by the sterling area. The recovery measures of a power with world interests would not readily agree with a program of European cooperation and integration, to use Paul Hoffman's phrase.

When in 1948 Britain presented her four-year recovery program to the Organization for European Economic

Cooperation, there were outraged cries from the Continent, especially from France. The plan was criticized as being "insular or imperial rather than European." One delegate said: "Britain had weighed anchor and sailed out of Europe."[9] The British plan called for heavy investments at home to increase production for exports and contemplated a reduction of imports in order to balance British accounts by 1953. In French eyes the consequences of the plan would mean that after Britain had cut down imports from France, the latter would be short of sterling.

Foreign Secretary Bevin gave a Socialist tone to his rejection of French criticism. "The fact is that there was a luxury market in this country in the 19th and 20th centuries. The French must appreciate that that luxury market has gone. . . . I therefore appeal to my friends in France to shape their economy to meet a necessity market."[10] The British Government indicated that it was prepared to buy increasing quantities of French agricultural produce and meat, but it was not ready to hitch its own planning to the optimistic goals of the French Monnet Plan.[11]

Another difficulty arose from the fact that the objective of recovery under the Marshall Plan tended to merge into the problem of ending dependence on dollar aid. This ob-

---

[9] *The Observer*, Nov. 6, 1948.

[10] This was followed by an apallingly painful interchange of remarks on French books. *Weekly Hansard*, House of Commons, No. 109, Dec. 9, 1948, clmn. 583. *The Times* nostalgically recalled that the British duty on a gallon of French light wines had been 1 shilling in 1859, 4 shillings in 1939 and was 25 shillings in 1949. "It would be easier if France were a cornucopia of snack and mousetrap cheese, but those useful antidotes to stark hunger are not within M. Schuman's power to dispense. Light wines are among the most important contributions that he can offer to the balance of Anglo-French trade." *The Times,* Jan. 22, 1949.

[11] This criticism was echoed in *The Observer,* Dec. 12, 1949: "But the plan is most optimistic, both in its estimate of increased production and in its programme of capital investment. It stands little chance of success without the most far-reaching fiscal reform in France."

jective drove the European states into restrictive courses, which clashed with the objective of unification and increased production.[21]

Marshall aid was flexibly administered, and, on the whole, the British government was well pleased with the machinery of the Organization for European Economic Cooperation. It involved the cooperation of sovereign governments, an approach to union which the British defined as functional. In part, this represented a British belief which arose from experience with the Commonwealth, a belief in growing together. In part, this insistence on a functional approach masked Britain's unwillingness to merge in a purely European Union, an unwillingness based on the fact that some of Britain's strongest ties of loyalty and support came from the Commonwealth. British refusal to accept the implications of European Union and integration raised three questions about the program.[13]

First of all, could a Union of Western Europe command the resources of strength and loyalty which the British kingdom could draw upon. The British were making heavy sacrifices to achieve solvency and strength. Would the same readiness serve a wider cause? Closer Union involved such touchy questions as standards of living, social security and taxation. Would not union compound mistrust and suspicions? Practically all Englishmen thought of France as a relatively undisciplined nation in civic and social matters, a land of tax evaders. If the even lower civic performance of Greece were considered, would not union bring

---

[12] J. K. Galbraith, "European Recovery: The Longer View," *The Review of Politics,* XII (April, 1950), 170.

[13] In reference to the Marshall Plan Bevin said that the United States was a great exponent of free enterprise at home and a wonderful planner for the outside world. Eden replied: "With us it is the other way round." *Weekly Hansard,* House of Commons, No. 109, Dec. 9, 1948, clmn. 582.

greater discord? Britain had fought and been weakened to stay independent. Sentiment for union was strongest among the formerly occupied and the vanquished.

Secondly, was Europe a sufficient basis for union? Certainly the efforts of Italy and France to establish a customs-union revealed little hope for economic progress through union alone. In the long run, by drastically recasting European economy, union might be feasible. But for short-run recovery the United States contribution to the Marshall Plan was proof enough that Europe by itself was inadequate. Even the immediate British hope of recovery was based on world trade, not on Europe alone.

The third question has, in part, been anticipated. Did not the degree of cooperation desired require an economic control council, and, along with it, a political structure? Could such a structure merely grow, as the British position suggested? The answer to that was certainly negative.[14]

European Union, then, presented genuine difficulties for Britain. The permanent officials of the British Foreign Office would certainly confront the Labour leaders with those difficulties. On the other hand, the Labour leaders themselves were not enthusiastic for union, and did not encourage the search for measures which would take account of Britain's difficulties and advance the cause of union. Because of Britain's negative and unimaginative role, other European nations did not always present their own difficulties with frankness and allowed Britain to bear the onus of opposing union. The particular difficulties which La-

---

[14] A very interesting series of articles on the relations between the British Commonwealth and European Union appeared in *The Round Table,* XXXVIII (1948), 517-544, 633-642, 742-761. The supporters of closer union (federal or otherwise) with Europe usually emphasized that the Commonwealth itself in foreign policy was regrettably lacking in cohesion.

bour's program and attitude created, were a reluctance to abate the sovereignty of national economic planning, and a mistrust of the liberal economic policies of the dominant parties in Western Europe. Labour's mistrust extended to the Socialist Parties of France and Italy, which Labour considered to be hopelessly doctrinaire. Scandinavian and Dutch Socialism was more to Labour's taste.[15] With a kind of saving inconsistency, Mr. Bevin sometimes expressed a personal preference for "liberal" measures, which conflicted with the demands of Socialist planning. On several occasions he favored the abolition of passports and complete freedom of travel.

Labour's nationalism when Labour was in power belied the internationalism of its traditional slogans. Mr. Churchill in supporting European Union noted that he was out of office but with masterly partisan deftness he held out the lofty vision of united Europe by quoting Prime Minister Attlee's pre-war statement; "Europe must federate or perish." Attlee said that, "and I have no reason to suppose that he will abandon that prescient declaration at a time when the vindication of his words is at hand."[16]

3. *Bevin Proposes Western Union and Secures a Military Alliance.*

In the face of considerable pressure Mr. Bevin on January 22, 1948, finally proposed Western Union. As West-

---

[15] Denis Healey, "The International Socialist Conference, 1946-1950," *International Affairs*, XXVI (1950), 363-373.

[16] Mr. Churchill did not so commit himself. His speeches convinced many that he was prepared for the broadest kind of European Union. But if they had been closely studied, the practical limits of his enthusiasm would have been evident. In his United Europe speech (May 14, 1947), he carefully distinguished between the British Empire and Commonwealth and "Europe, with which Great Britain is profoundly blended." Churchill, *Europe Unite* (London, 1950), pp. 84, 79.

ern Union had been initially proposed by the Conservatives, its advocacy was politically embarrassing for Bevin. But Western Union could also be proposed in a Third Force guise, as a measure to create a European power bloc, independent of the Soviet Union and the United States.[17]

Bevin prefaced his proposal by recalling the three principles of his foreign policy. "The first is that no one nation should dominate Europe. The second is that the old fashioned conception of the balance of power as an aim should be discarded if possible. The third is that there be substituted Four-Power cooperation and assistance to all the states of Europe, to enable them to evolve freely each in its own way."[18] International agreement had not been allowed to work. Europe was not allowed to work together,

---

[17] The Labour Party pamphlet, "Feet on the Ground" (London, 1948), p. 5. Shortly before Bevin espoused Western Union, G. D. H. Cole again urged the establishment of an international Socialist organization of European economic life. Only such an arrangement would permit Europe to grow in strength and to be a genuine "middle force" between the Communist and Capitalist giants." Cole admitted that the resources of the United States enabled it to make capitalism work. G. D. H. Cole, "Democratic Socialism for Europe" *New Statesman & Nation* (Jan. 17, 1948), 43-44. Churchill addressing the Congress of Europe, placed European Union within the framework of his long-range program. "The design for world government might have followed the system of three or more groups of armies—in this case armies of peace—under one supreme headquarters. Thus I saw the vast Soviet Union forming one of these great groups. The Council of Europe, including Great Britain linked with her Empire and Commonwealth, would be another. Thirdly there was the United States and her sister republics in the Western Hemisphere." If such a scheme had been followed these regional associations would have settled "a greater number of differences and difficulties, which are now dragged up to the supreme world organization." Under such an arrangement "far fewer, but also far more potent figures would represent them at the summit. There was also the hope that they would meet not in an overcrowded Tower of Babel, but, as it were, upon a mountain top where all was cool and quiet and calm, and from which the wide vision of the world would be presented with all things in their due proportion." Churchill, *Europe Unite,* pp. 314-315. Shades of Yalta!

[18] *Weekly Hansard,* House of Commons, No. 75, January 22, 1948, clmn. 390.

for "in Eastern Europe we are presented with a *fait accompli*" and in Greece with a "case of power politics."[19] Bevin recited the whole catalogue of disagreements with the Soviet Union from Germany and Austria to Japan. Thus, Bevin's third principle was impractical and the balance of power could not be wholly discarded. Disagreement had come to a head with the Marshall Plan. "This programme brought vividly to light what must have been under the surface, and what was responsible for these attitudes ever since the war, and, if I may say so, for some of the events we had to face during the war."[20]

This brewing hostility revealed itself in the Paris negotiations on the Marshall Plan, when the Soviet Union refused participation and "preferred to risk the Western Plan or Western Union—that is to say, they risked the creation of any possible organism in the West. My further opinion is that they thought they could wreck or intimidate Western Europe by political upsets, economic chaos and even revolutionary methods." As evidence of this, Bevin cited the founding of the Cominform and the political strikes in France.[21]

The added failure of the London Conference on Germany makes clear that "we have to face a new situation . . . surely all these developments which I have been describing point to the conclusion that the free nations of Western Europe must now draw closely together."[22] But, after Bevin had enumerated the difficulties and reservations of his proposal, it is not surprising that Western Union largely resulted in a military alliance, the Brussels Treaty (March, 1948). This treaty bound Britain, France, Belgium, the Netherlands and Luxemburg to give "all the military and

---

[19] *Ibid.,* clmns. 409, 386, 387.
[20] *Ibid.,* clmn. 389.
[21] *Ibid.,* clmns. 394-395.
[22] *Ibid.,* clmn. 397.

other aid and assistance in their power," if any one of them should be "the object of an armed attack in Europe." This Western European defense agreement was an earnest of good intentions which made possible the later North Atlantic Treaty. Britain had again approached Europe as the seat of a greatly weakened Grand Alliance. But her world interests deterred her from the closer union for which many Europeans had hoped.

Bevin denied that the British approach to Europe was, in the tradition of British diplomacy, largely military. He frequently recalled the Treaty's provision for other kinds of functional cooperation. In May, 1948, speaking to the Labour Party Conference at Scarborough, Bevin stated that his speech on Western Union had been delivered after the Cabinet had approved the policy. "Subsequently we made a treaty with the interested nations. In that treaty there are very interesting functions. All the treaties I have studied hitherto have been just pure alliances. We decided as a Cabinet to try and make this one a functional treaty." He recalled that he had proposed the initially futile Military Committee of the United Nations. He continued to hope for the extension of Western Union so that it could become a true measure of collective security. It would then appear to be such and no longer be subject to the interpretation that it was for the United States and against the Soviet Union.[23]

One year after his Western Union propoal Bevin, addressing the Foreign Press Association in London (January 25, 1949), surveyed the year's work and described British policy for the future. "I would regard it as a crowning event to establish European unity on a sound, definite, and pro-

---

[23] *Report of the 47th Conference of the Labour Party* (London, 1948), pp. 197-198.

gressive basis." The objective of this unity,[24] as he conceived it, was twofold: to restore a decent standard of life and a chance of contentment to the European people, who had experienced the devastations of Hitler's armies; and to establish a great and unaggressive organism, so that "others would recognize that power and there would be a reasonable chance of peace in the world." The United Nations had been a great disappointment in matters of defense and security, but such a European organization might supplement the United Nations and make it effective.

Bevin indicated that he was unable to explain the unwillingness of the Soviet Union to participate in this constructive work. He appeared to believe that it was due to Marxism or "the Lenin theory"—a "wretched ideological difficulty." The Foreign Secretary assumed the mantle of the practical Englishman and tried to rally all reasonable men to the constructive work of raising living standards, for "argument was no answer to Communism." He therefore welcomed Truman's Point Four Program of assistance to underdeveloped areas and promised to pool British skills and resources with the Program.

In discussing the prospects of union Mr. Bevin became more obscure and, actually, ran counter to the experience which he had had with functional union in Germany. "The only way to deal with sovereignty was to build up slowly a greater sovereignty in which all others were merged." For his functional approach Bevin cited his own experience in merging forty-seven trade unions into one. Actually, his instance seemed to favor the political union, although, perhaps, he meant to suggest that political union would temporarily distract Europe from issues which required immediate attention. "If one could achieve exchange of travel and

---

[24] *The Times,* January 26, 1949.

100

organization of basic industries on a European basis, it would go a long way to creating the kind of economic basis that made possible the political union."

Bevin presented his functionalism as a practical approach which avoided "theoretical escapism" and promises doomed to disappointment. He wanted no rabbit-like multiplication of European agencies and talking shops. His ultimate objective was "a practical organism in Europe in which we should cease to be English or French or other nationality, and would be Europeans, with an organization that would carry out a European policy in the face of new developments in the world."

But, pending this European development, Britain had to proclaim her special character as "the cornerstone of a great commonwealth, and new development in Asia must be linked with Western Union. He believed that the freedom Britain had given to India, Burma and Ceylon, would not result in division between East and West, but an indivisible union between all."[25]

4. *The German Problem as an Incentive to European Union*

In American and British eyes, Germany passed through a transition from a frustrating spoil of victory into a major contributor to the plans for European Recovery. The new bizonal policy in Germany was set forth —by General Clay in a directive (July 11, 1947). The goal was "the attainment at the earliest practicable date of a self-sustaining German economy." Meanwhile, German public opinion was becoming important. It was clear that a German government would have to be established to gain the effective cooperation of the German people. The United States and Britain did reduce Potsdam limitations on German produc-

---

[25] *The Times*, Jan. 26, 1949.

tion but they were unwilling to organize Germany in any way which would cause them to bear the onus of dividing the nation. At Moscow the Foreign Ministers had agreed again to meet at London. Until that meeting failed, an energetic approach to German unification was not politically wise.[26]

The Moscow meeting had revealed some agreement about a provisional constitution but no accord upon the economic conditions for an eventually self-supporting Germany. The London meeting resulted in the same impasse, although the limitation on German steel capacity was raised to 12 million tons. Molotov proposed that the first task should be to provide a central government for Germany. When the territorial extent of that government was raised, Molotov insisted that the Oder-Neisse line could not be discussed. Moreover, Molotov refused to approve the economic integration of the Saar into France.

All arguments for the economic unity of Germany and for the Allied contention that the first charge on German exports should be for the payment of imports were countered by the Russian demand for reparations of $10 billion. The Russians were not even prepared to indicate how much they had taken from Germany until the amount claimed had been conceded. At Moscow and London the Russians believed that they would profit from waiting.

---

[26] Speaking to the Labour Party Conference (May 29, 1947) Bevin said that the bizonal arrangement was not a final division of Germany but "a temporary expedient forced upon us by the refusal of other powers to agree to the genuine economic unity of the whole country." General Clay reports this agreement with Sir Brian Robertson on the necessity of making the Executive Committee of the German Economic Council into "something very close to a government. . . . However, we felt it undesirable to proceed further or more rapidly pending the outcome of the next meeting of the Council of Foreign Ministers which was to convene in London." Clay, *Decision in Germany,* p. 175.

After the end of the London Conference (Nov-Dec., 1947) Bevin said: "Our experience at Moscow and our experience here . . . makes us wonder whether the Council of Foreign Ministers will ever be able to settle the European and German problems."[27] He again expressed his weariness with Soviet speeches and accusations. "I made it clear that if there is to be no settlement between the Four Powers we cannot go on forever with the burden of cost this represents, with Western Europe in chaos, and with no means of redress." The Marshall Plan made him more hopeful in his firm opposition to the Soviet Union. "We cannot go on as we have been going on. . . . We shall close no doors. . . . Meanwhile we are going to push on to raise the German standard of life." Eden clarified the obscurity of Bevin's speech: "There is now no choice open to us but to do everything in our power to promote recovery in that part of Europe where we are still free to act—that is to say, Western Europe."[28]

This disagreement was final. There remained the problem of joining the French Zone to the Anglo-American Zones. In turn, this involved a settlement of the Ruhr problem. The British had planned to nationalize the Ruhr mines but there was a dispute about the identity of the authority to whom the nationalization should be granted. France was eager to place the Ruhr under an international authority. The United States was reluctant to approve nationalization. As the United States (Dec. 17, 1947) agreed to accept major financial responsibility for German imports, its proposal that the disposition of ownership be left to the German people was accepted. Bevin was able to score against

---

[27] *The Times,* May 23, 1949.
[28] *Weekly Hansard,* House of Commons, No. 74, December 18, 1947, clmns. 1883-1889.

his critics by noting that there was Four Power agreement on allowing the German people to consider socialization.[29]

The United States called the tune but British policy was in considerable agreement. Western Germany was to be unified economically and to that end was to be allowed a large measure of self-government. These objectives were expressed in General Sir Brian Robertson's speech at Dusseldorf on April 7. "We must accept as a fact that an iron curtain splits Germany. For the time being we must be content with unity so far as it can be achieved, and do not forget that this means the unity of two-thirds of Germany."[30]

The outlines of the future became clearer. The British and Americans were prepared to move ahead and establish a German government. This objective was in the interest of economy and recovery. But these interests required French cooperation. France, however, suffered from two fears. The first was the fear that the objective of recovery would be used to justify the priority of German development over French. The second was the general fear of German aggression. The Benelux countries did not share the first French fear, for their economic life was more dependent on German recovery. France, however, found her own interests in security at odds with American-British proposals. French statesmen were not able to move quickly, for the French Assembly closely and heatedly watched German developments. They saw the necessity of German recovery but believed that the Anglo-American timetable placed recovery before security. French objections were sometimes mediated by Britain, which generally did not differ from the United States. During 1948 Congressional approval of Marshall

---

[29] *Weekly Hansard,* House of Commons, No. 74, Dec. 18, 1947, clmns. 1891-1892.

[30] Quoted in John C. Campbell, *The United States in World Affairs, 1948-1949* (New York, 1949), p. 73.

Aid offered France an inducement for compromise. In June, 1948, a London meeting secured French agreement to an International Ruhr Authority, which was to supervise and allocate the area's industrial production. The British and Americans were mindful of French objections to the centralization of Germany. French concern for security persisted in all the delicate arrangements for the Ruhr until a more thorough going security arrangement appeared in the North Atlantic Treaty.

Another current in French policy appeared, a current which awakened responses in Germany. Robert Schuman in opposing Anglo-American policy on the ownership of Ruhr industries (December 2, 1948) said that the "Europeanization of Ruhr coal and steel" is the only means of reconciling the requirements of European security with a balanced German economy. He described France's objective as the preparation of "the admission of Germany to a peaceful and democratic organization of the European nations, on condition that Germany's restoration is held within such limits that any threat of German hegemony is excluded."[31]

French objections to German ownership or management of the Ruhr mines ran counter to the objective of recovery. German recovery required a considerable measure of German participation and the eventual transfer of the government of Germany to German hands. Actually, ownership was not the decisive issue, which was that "Germany . . . will become a great power again—unless by that time she is merged in some supranational community of Powers."[32] At the be-

---

[31] Parts of the speech are given in *Chronology of International Events & Documents,* IV (no. 23), November 19-December 9, 1948, pp. 794-795, and in *The Observer,* Dec. 5, 1948.

[32] *The Observer,* Nov. 14, 1948. Paul Reynaud said that European Union was necessary to create a wide market for European-made goods and to contain and direct the strength of Germany. *The Observer,* Jan. 9, 1949.

ginning of 1949 the British Military Governor told the German people: "This year will bring the formation of a German Government and greatly increase opportunities for Germans to take part in the arrangement of their country's affairs."[33] Meanwhile, the Minister-President of North Rhine—Westphalia, in criticizing the unilateral and unwelcome control of the Ruhr, made a counter-proposal which paralleled Schuman's earlier remarks. He proposed the establishment of a "utility association under international law on co-operative lines. Germany would contribute the Ruhr, France the ore deposits of Lorraine, both countries those of the Saar, and Belgium and Luxemburg their heavy industries. If this idea were thought out consistently, France could feel assured that the industrial potential of the Ruhr would never again be abused for purposes contrary to an all-European conception."[34]

The dynamics of allowing the Germans self-government moved fast. The British and American governments had to recognize that concessions had to be made to the democratic German parties or these would be derided as puppets of the occupation forces.[35]

In the eighteen months after the London Conference of Foreign Ministers (1947) West Germany began to emerge as a functioning state. The blockade of Berlin had gained support for British and American policies. When the blockade was halted, the Soviet Union took the initiative in calling a new meeting of the Conference of Foreign Ministers at Paris (May, 1949). The Soviet objective was to prevent the incorporation of Germany into the Western Community. Vyshinsky proposed on May 24 a return to Potsdam and a

[33]   *The Observer,* Jan. 2, 1949.
[34]   *The Observer,* Jan. 9, 1949.
[35]   *The Times,* April 8, 1949.

union of the eastern and western zones under the Allied Control Council. Bevin rejected the Soviet proposal, and emphasized the fact that Britain had been prepared to operate Potsdam and had changed only after Russian policy had threatened to turn Germany into a "cesspool of starvation."

The leaders of the new German Federal Republic were opposed to German rearmament. This stand was taken both on principle and on interest, for an independent German army was feared in all democratic quarters in Germany. Speaking to an American newsman Chancellor Adenauer also pointed to a course on which Germany could join France. "If the allies demand that we should take part in the defence of western Europe, I should be in favor, not of an independent Wehrmacht but of a German contingent in a European force."[36] Adenauer steered a skillful and enlightened course. Thus, he had to express his opposition to the French position on the Saar, though he tempered it with the judgment that the creation of Europe was more important for all Europeans, including the Germans, than the Saar problem alone.[37]

Meanwhile the British again sought to mediate. General Robertson told a German audience: "Good relations between France and Germany are a precondition of good relations between England and Germany."[38]

5. *The European Community and the Atlantic Community.*

By 1949 European Union had become more imperative from the standpoint of security than from that of recovery. The logic of disagreement, meanwhile, had engulfed the Brussels Treaty in the North Atlantic Treaty Organization

---

[36]   *The Times,* Dec. 5, 1949.
[37]   *The Times,* Jan. 17, 1950.
[38]   *The Times,* January 18, 1950.

(April 4, 1949). The bringing of the United States and Canada into the European defense system allayed Britain's concern about the inadequacies of the Brussels Treaty. For the future it promised the creation of strength, although the emphasis was more on recovery than on armaments.[39] Britain, moreover, now felt more secure, and, with the military problem approaching an apparent solution, was all the less disposed to European Union. On the Continent, however, Germany's approach to sovereignty and her destined part in European recovery and ultimate defense, made the merger of Germany into a European Community all the more imperative.

On this issue, the stark limits of Bevin's espousal of the cause of union were revealed. Britain with its world interests welcomed N.A.T.O because it meant embracing Europe within a wider community. The Atlantic Community was more spacious and did not make the stern demands for union which the European community did. The island position of Britain and its widely dispersed interests made it difficult for Britain to think about Europe in the same geographic terms as France did. In spite of, and, perhaps, because of Indo-China, France was a power whose vital interests focussed on Germany and Mediterranean Africa. France also had

---

[39] Mr. Bevin, in announcing the conclusion of the agreement, stressed the purely defensive character of the alliance, which, bringing Western Europe "under a wider roof of security," brought Britain into defensive alliance with the United States without weakening Britain's obligations to the Commonwealth and other states. The confidence inspired by the Pact would enable a more rapid economic development. Mr. Warbey, a Labour M.P., opposed the Pact as a fundamental change in policy, a departure "even from the policy which the Prime Minister and the Foreign Secretary themselves enunciated of an independent third group of nations which was not tied to either of the two super world powers." This Pact was a military alliance and would divide the world into two hostile camps. He understood Conservative support for the Pact, "because it indeed represents the fulfillment of the aims of" Mr. Churchill. *Weekly Hansard*, House of Commons, No. 120, March 18, 1949, clmns. 2544-2550.

some hope of making European Union the nucleus of an independent force in world affairs. Britain refused to jeopardize its world interests by merging in such a community. The obscurity of Foreign Secretary Bevin's initial advocacy of Western Union may have been calculated. Indeed, his failure to implement it in any but a military way may have been a masterpiece of "intelligent inaction" until, to Britain's satisfaction and the benefit of Europe, the new world again came in to redress the balance of the old.[40]

The Brussels Treaty, as a military alliance, did not satisfy the aspirations of the various European Unity movements which in May, 1948, met as the European Congress at the Hague. This Congress, which was not popular in the British Labour Party, urged the governments to convene a European Assembly to begin the work of unification. In August, 1948, Belgium and France submitted proposals for such an Assembly to the Permanent Commission of the Union of Western Europe.

The British Government firmly refused to create an authority above itself, and this was the apparent objective of Belgium and France. The latter country sent a delegation of elder statesmen to the Constituent Assembly (at Paris). Britain sent only representatives of the Government. After lengthy and acrimonious sessions, a compromise (May 5, 1949) was established. Britain abandoned its insistence that the European Union be limited to a Council of Ministers and direct representatives of governments. To the Council of Ministers was added an Assembly consisting of representatives of each member country. Each representative was to have one vote and was not to be bound by goverment instructions. A British White Paper (June 21, 1949) explained: "The Assembly will not merely reflect the main

---

[40] "France and Britain," *The Observer*, Dec. 12, 1948.

groups of public opinion in the member countries, it should also in its debates create and formulate an European opinion, and in its recommendations tender united European advice to member governments."

Again, in spite of and because of Bevin's objections, "a talking shop" or forum of European public opinion was created. But as the Council's history later revealed, public opinion without political power is not very effective. The frustration of the Assembly by the Council of Ministers increased European irritation with Britain.

Mr. Bevin, who in departing from his prepared briefs sometimes expressed his thoughts with startling frankness, clearly did not find European Union adequate. To the House of Commons he replied to an unfriendly question: "I have often said that I amalgamated a lot of unions into one union, but the first thing I looked at was the assets."[41] He then gave a clear expression of British difficulties in the way of Union and sketched the line of development for which he hoped. "I feel that the intricacies of Western Europe are such that we had better proceed—I am not dogmatic about this—on the same principle of association of nations that we have in the Commonwealth. Britain has to be in both places; she has to be and must remain the centre of the Commonwealth itself and she must be European. It is a very difficult role to play. It is different from that of anyone else and I think that adopting the principle of an unwritten constitution, and the process of constant association step by step, by treaty and agreement and by taking on certain things collectively instead of by ourselves, is the right way to approach this Western Union problem."[42]

---

[41] *Weekly Hansard,* House of Commons, No. 101, Sept. 15, 1948, clmn. 105. An opponent replied: "Jolly good capitalism."

[42] *Ibid.,* clmn. 106. See Churchill's speech October 9, 1948, to the Conservative Conference at Llandudno.

Later (1949) before his Labour Party colleagues he defended Western Union as the alternative to the failure of Great Power cooperation. In Foreign affairs "you cannot plan in quite the same way and with the same assurance of the path you will follow as in domestic affairs."[43] This note of uncertainty was to be sounded in greater volume, as the logic of disagreement worked itself out in later challenges. It also expressed a sense of weakness, which excused the uncreative role of Britain in balancing her world interests against the demands of geography and European Union.

---

[43] *Report of the 48th Annual Conference of the Labour Party* (London, 1949), p. 187.

111

CHAPTER FIVE

Crises in European Union and the Atlantic Community

"Defence, however, is of much more importance than opulence."
Adam Smith (1776).

"I am looking for peace. I am looking for a way to stop war, but you will not stop it by sentiments and appeals. You will stop it only by making practical arrangements."
Winston Churchill (1936).

By the summer of 1949 Britain was committed to the defense of Western Europe by the Brussels Treaty, and to the defense of the Atlantic Community by the North Atlantic Treaty. But, in spite of the existence of a Western European command Headquarters under Marshall Montgomery, the military organization of Western Europe was far from formidable.

The logic of disagreement demonstrated that the promised and prospective assistance of an alliance was insufficient. The Alliance required an army. The succeeding year was to see a progressive revelation of the strength of the Soviet Union and its satellites and a parallel realization of Western Europe's weakness. Britain's military commitments were confined to Europe, but, in the face of American and European pressure for closer union with the Continent, Britain tirelessly pointed to her world interests. These world interests, in turn, provoked a clash with American policy over the consequences of United Nations resistance to North Korean aggression. The American decision provided the impetus to a new emphasis on armaments, if necessary at the expense of recovery. Until the North Korean aggression, however, strength through recovery was the dominant theme. In May, 1950, the foreign ministers of Britain, France and the United States, meeting in London, announced agreement on the necessity of achieving at the same time "full maintenance of social and material standards" and "adequate development of necessary defense measures."[1] Strength through recovery, however, was not the same as armed strength in being. Initially, the possible conflict of the two objectives was ignored, or nicely obscured by talk about balanced forces. Even in the United States it appeared that the creation of positions of strength was more a slogan than an immediate objective. In the second half of 1950 the objectives of recovery and of armed strength began to diverge and to add new problems to the conflicts and contradictions of earlier policies.

1. *Conflict of British Recovery and European Cooperation.*

Under the Organization for European Economic Cooperation Britain was pledged to work for increased production, internal financial stability and the reduction of barriers to multilateral trade. In addition, the United States looked for larger gestures of cooperation and some progress towards the integration of European economies. These were not forthcoming. Britain used her Marshall Plan aid to good effect, but not to the end of integrating her economy with Europe. Britain was prepared to work with other sovereign states, but was opposed to any abrogation of sovereignty for the sake of a merely European integration. Even a move to

---

[1] *The Observer,* May 14, 1950.

113

appoint a director general over the O.E.E.C. was opposed by Britain, for such an officer might have dominated the authority of the individual states. Significantly enough, the British functional approach approved an alternative proposal, the naming of a "political conciliator."[2] The last months of 1949 were days of almost unrelieved gloom in O.E.E.C. circles, who found union impossible while Britain played the part of a floating island, at one moment in sight of Europe, and later, far out of sight. In prospect, the dollar shortage was certain to continue.[3] Baron Snoy, Chairmain of O.E.E.C., and M. Marjolin its Secretary-General,, reported: "We have paid very special attention to Britain's position not only in view of the welfare of the populations of the sterling area, but also because of the immense part played by the sterling area in the European and world economy. This is a problem for which our organization can find no solution, but to which it was our duty to draw particular attention."[4]

a. DEVALUATION AND ITS CONSEQUENCES IN EUROPE AND THE WORLD

By the summer of 1949 Britain, faced by the rapid depletion of its gold and dollar reserves, confronted the problem with measures which, for a time, stalled even the talk of European cooperation.

---

[2] *The Times,* Feb. 1, 1950, described this office as "a new post designed to permit effective and constant leadership."

[3] "On the European side there has always been considerable fogginess about what, in concrete terms, nineteen more or less bankrupt nations could contribute to each other." *The Economist,* CLVII (Oct. 29, 1949), 932. This article is a good example of the pessimism in which *The Economist* occasionally indulges.

[4] *New York Times,* Sept. 2, 1949, Paul Van Zeeland said: "I am not satisfied with the way the O.E.E.C. has done its job. Instead of coordinating Europe in the economic field, all the organization did was to distribute dollars." *The Times,* Nov. 14, 1947.

The difficulties in Britain's progress to recovery again revealed the slender margin on which Britain supported a program of social welfare and defense preparations.[5] Britain's industrial production was advancing steadily, and her exports for the first quarter of 1949 amounted to 156% of the 1938 level. There was no unemployment and no obvious slack to pick up. The trade volume was satisfactory but its direction was wrong. Britain and the sterling area were not selling enough goods to the dollar area to pay for dollar imports. A brief and small decline in the United States economy intensified the dollar shortage, for British exports to the United States declined as did American purchases of raw material from the sterling area. In the second quarter of 1949 the gold and dollar deficit of the sterling area doubled the first quarter's deficit to reach $628,000,000. In July, Britain and the Commonwealth drastically reduced dollar purchases, but the shortage continued. The Chancellor of the Exchequer, Sir Stafford Cripps, insisted that these were necessary but negative measures. A solution required the sterling area to increase the volume of its sales to the dollar area.[6] Provision for this was made in a conference at Washington in September. The communique of this conference expressed the agreement of the United States and Canada to reduce "obstacles to the entry of goods and services from debtor countries, in order to provide as wide an opportunity as possible for those countries to earn dollars."[7]

---

[5] Somewhat despairingly an American official put the situation to James Reston in the following terms: "The British for months now have been very much like the clown in the circus whose full-dress suit looked fairly reliable but could be zipped right off his body by stepping on a hidden string." *The New York Times*, Feb. 26, 1950.

[6] *Weekly Hansard,* House of Commons, No. 132, July 6, 1949, clmn. 2162.

[7] *Department of State Bulletin,* XXI (Sept. 26, 1949), 473-75.

In the Washington talks, a decisive element in Britain's lack of dollars, the sterling balances, was scheduled for later consideration. Where these obligations existed, British manufacturers found an easy market. Thus, many British exporters did not have a sufficient incentive to embark on the necessary but risky course of trying to sell in hard currency areas. "Unrequited exports" to such countries as India and Pakistan were represented by the British Government as a contribution to Asian recovery. These exports also served to maintain British commercial interests. The United States government, however, regarded these balances as a source of Britain's economic weakness. In April, 1950, a British memorandum, which linked American aid to Asia with a reduction of the sterling balances, was disclosed by Senator Tom Connally, who criticized it sharply and, in effect, ended all serious consideration of the subject.

Fortified by an American agreement to reduce tariffs and to consider stockpiling purchases, Cripps on September 18, 1949, announced the devaluation of the pound from $4.03 to $2.80. This decision, taken without consulting Britain's European Allies, was an irritating assertion of Britain's detachment from Europe and of her special association with the United States. There may have been good reason for this refusal to consult, for Britain had dark suspicions about French behavior in the earlier convertibility crisis. Nevertheless, the unilateral action angered France, whose Finance Minister, M. Petsche, called the devaluation a "trade-war rate." In other countries, for example Egypt, the reaction was also sharp and bitter.

The British action did not promote cooperation or an atmosphere conducive to it. It strengthened the suspicion that European Union, functional or any other kind, was not a firm British objective. Mr. Bevin's frequent assertion that he would deal with every problem on its merits, also seemed to indicate the same indecisiveness.[8]

Devaluation was attempted without regard for Europe, because of Britain's world sterling interests. Many of these, however, were also adversely affected by devaluation, notably Argentina. Here, economic nationalism met economic nationalism head on. After devaluation the Argentine Government increased its asking price for a ton of meat from £97.55 to £140. The British Government, declaring the original price too high, offered £90 a ton. Government bulk-buying of Argentine meat and wheat transferred these commercial negotiations into diplomatic duels in which the Argentina of Peron bargained hard, and British officials uttered cries of "blackmail." Moreover, the sharp practices of the Argentine government's exchange transactions at the expense of Argentine meat producers created domestic strains which had to be directed against Britain. In truth, Britain's bargaining position was not favorable. She needed the meat and could not supply Argentina with sufficient coal, steel and oil. Moreover, Britain paid in sterling, which was not convertible into dollars.[9] The need of scape-goats and villains, when diplomatic difficulties resulted in a reduced meat ra-

---

[8] To the Canadian Club in Ottawa Mr. Bevin described British policy: "We must continue to examine problems as they arise, anticipate those likely to arise and make arrangements to meet them." *The Economist,* CLVII (Oct. 8, 1949), 762-763, commented: "But is this enough? A policy which moves from problem to problem and from expedient to expedient, may wander off its true course even without its framers noticing that the deviation has occurred. This, rather than perfidy, explains Britain's apparent lack of enthusiasm for Western Cooperation . . . the contingencies of day-to-day events are not related to broad policy, for the policy does not exist."

[9] The Argentine Secretary of State for Economic Affairs, Dr. Ares, reminded Britain that she could not hope to buy primary products cheaply, while manufactured goods were dear. *The Times,* March 4, 1949. Even before devaluation, Argentina had deliberately failed to meet the meat quotas provided for in the Miranda Treaty of 1948. A British spokesman called this non-fulfillment of the Treaty *force-majeure. The Times,* March 5, 1949.

117

tion, puts a peculiarly heavy burden on diplomacy. Under earlier agreements Britain had agreed to allow the Argentine government to buy up the British controlled railways in Argentina. Devaluation, however, interrupted the operation of the five-year trade treaty signed in July, 1949, and eventually caused the drastic reduction of the British meat ration in late 1950 and early 1951.[10]

b. Liberalizing Trade and Currency Exchange.

Devaluation, then, injured the cause of cooperation. Britain, however, did contribute to the reduction of trade barriers. Many import quotas were removed and for numerous goods the requirement of government permits was abolished. In the larger field of world trade Britain participated in the formulation of the Havana Trade Charter, but has followed America's lead in failing to ratify it. Britain provisionally accepted the General Agreement on Tariffs and Trade (Geneva, 1947). The search for wider agreement at Torquay (1950-51) produced considerable acrimony, and again the stumbling block of Britain's Imperial Preferences remained firm.[11]

The British Government was also a party to the O.E.E.C.'s attempts to make the currencies of Western Europe convertible. But Britain was determined to oppose any effort to make the currency freely convertible into dollars.

---

[10] In June, 1950, the Argentine Senate affirmed Argentine sovereignty over the Falkland Islands.

The details of Britain's trade treaties and financial agreements are usefully summarized in the quarterly issues of the *Midland Bank Review*.

[11] For an analysis of the Charter, see J. E. S. Fawcett, "The Havana Charter" in *The Year Book of World Affairs, 1951* (London, 1951), pp. 269-289.

At the same time, it must be remembered that the United States spoke with two voices. The voice of policy favored the widest liberalizing of trade. The voice of practice, Congressional action, was sometimes restrictionist.

A second difficulty was that Britain's part in the European Payments Union was based on Europe's trade with the whole sterling area, and not with Britain in Europe alone. In other words, Britain insisted that special provisions be made for sterling as an international currency. A British proposal in March, 1950, designed to protect that position, was particularly technical.[12] The British were in favor of superseding earlier bilateral by multilateral payments through a clearing house, but were opposed to the Belgian desire for an early revival of gold payments.

As the terms of British trade at the time were favorable, the British position appeared less self-interested than the Belgian one. At any rate, the promise of American dollar support for the European Payments Union Fund carried the day. The Union was agreed to later but applied to the period after July 1, 1950. With it the Marshall Countries reached "a freer flow of trade and payments than had been known since the war and—if Germany be included—possibly since the Great Depression."[13]

2. *Europe's Renewed Drive for Union.*

Progress towards union, apart from military alliance, was confined to the liberalization of trade and the limited convertibility of currencies. The British considered this substantial progress. Many Europeans, however, found these measures inadequate and sought assurance in the wider unity of a Europe which transcended and could override the sovereign states. To these people, the negative attitude of Mr.

---

[12] "Only three persons in London understand it," a half-serious Treasury official remarked to John Allan May. *Christian Science Monitor*, March 22, 1950. There is a useful commentary in *The New York Times*, May 21, 1950.

[13] Barbara Ward, *Policy for the West* (New York, 1951), pp. 240-241. Her account of the European Payments Union is admirably lucid. Cf., "The European Payments Union" in *The World Today*, VI (Nov., 1950), 490-498.

Bevin suggested that the functional approach was a veto of federalism, dressed in characteristic British empiricism. Britain, again, appeared to be seeking a middle way, where there was no middle. As the Catholics insisted that the Anglican Church was Protestant, so the federalist insisted that the functional approach in theory was old sovereignty writ large. To those intent on European Union, Britain's Commonwealth ties were a perpetual fog bank cutting England off from the Continent. There was a widespread and profound discouragement in France and in Western Europe generally.[14] A committee of the Council of Europe passed a resolution seeking information concerning the attitude of the British Commonwealth towards European Union. This represented an attempt to challenge Britain for using the Commonwealth ties as an excuse for negation and inaction in Europe.[15]

a. BRITISH RESERVE AND DOMESTIC POLITICS.

A number of things may explain this negative spirit. First of all, Mr. Bevin was unwell. It was a sad commentary on the Labour Party's factionalism and lack of new leaders that a satisfactory successor could not be found. Mr. Bevin's creative talents appear to have ended after his rather obscure espousal of Western Union in 1948.[16] This uncreativeness was reenforced by Bevin's awareness that Britain, as a rule, could not take an independent course on important mat-

---

[14] An excellent presentation of the British approach is in two articles by Sir Arthur Salter, *The Times,* May 16 and 17, 1950.

[15] *The Times,* December 22, 1949. Paul-Henri Spaak made the request in August, 1949. Bevin, after conferring with the Commonwealth ministers at Colombo, answered: "There need be no inconsistencies between the policy followed by the British Government with the Council of Europe and the British Government with its Commonwealth members." *Christian Science Monitor,* March 24, 1950. This was British reserve with a vengeance.

[16] This point is well expressed in an article, "Mr. Bevin's Record," in *The Economist,* CLVII (Dec. 17, 1949), 1331-1332.

ters.[17] But instead of drawing from this the lesson that Britain must be ingenious in devising measures and means of collaboration, after the signing of the North Atlantic Treaty, he took refuge in dispirited inaction.

This negative spirit was fostered by the British electorate's preoccupation with domestic affairs. In the parliamentary elections (Feb., 1950) foreign policy was considered only in the general terms of peace and war.[18] Churchill described the campaign as "demure."[19] The Conservatives contributed to this quietude, for they approved the broad outlines of Bevin's policy. This, in turn, caused difficulties for Labour's Foreign Secretary. The power of Mr. Churchill's personality revived the spectre of the continuity of British policy. Several times during the campaign Bevin felt compelled to deny that he took advice from the Conservative leader. Wearily he objected to the belief that "whenever he did anything good, it was because Mr. Churchill told him to do it." "I just want to correct this rather stupid impression that I have no initiative and no capacity."[20]

Bevin's discomfited apology was elicited by Churchill's masterly campaign speech at Edinburgh, where the Conservative leader approvingly noted that Bevin "has followed with steadfastness the line I marked out at Fulton of fraternal association with the United States and the closest unification of our military arrangements." He complimented Bevin for espousing, "albeit somewhat sheepishly," the cause

---

[17] Bevin, in answer to Eden's call for a declaration of British policy, said: "I hope to show that the day when we, as Great Britain, can declare a policy independently of our allies and colleagues has gone." *Weekly Hansard*, House of Commons, No. 149, March 28, 1950, clmn. 318.

[18] H. G. Nichols, *The British General Election of 1950* (London, 1951); Carl F. Brand, "The British General Election of 1950," *The South Atlantic Quarterly*, L (1951), 478-498; Peter G. Richards, "The General Election," *The Political Quarterly*, XXI (1950), 114-121.

[19] *The Times*, February 22, 1950.

[20] *The Times*, Feb. 21 and Feb. 22, 1950.

of United Europe. He recalled that a formidable world now dwarfed Britain, which no longer had controlling power or sufficient influence. Then, approaching the final proclamation of his own superiority to Bevin, he expressed the "earnest hope that we may find our way to some more exalted and august foundation for our safety than this grim and sombre balancing power of the [atom] bomb." Finally, as his expression of his superiority and his rejection of Labour's charge of warmongering, he suggested "the idea of another talk with Soviet Russia upon the highest level."[21]

Bevin replied that this was a stunt proposal and that the personal approach had notably failed at Munich and Yalta.[22] In answer, Churchill reasserted his own superiority and that Bevin's answer showed how far his mind dwelt below the true level of events.[23] Churchill's Edinburgh proposal had "rolled round the world. . . . It was clear to most people that more vision than Mr. Bevin possesses is required in the handling of our foreign affairs."[24]

Thereafter, Bevin never was able to take the initiative.[25]

Nevertheless, Churchill's boast that his proposal had dominated the election was belied by the results. The Labour Party won but its majority in the House of Commons was extremely small. The Labour Government, therefore,

---

[21] *The Times,* Feb. 15, 1950. Churchill phrased this suggestion very carefully. It was an idea, not a promise. Moreover, he fully protected himself; "I have not, of course, access to the secret information of the Government, nor am I fully informed about the attitude of the United States." It was a peculiarly dexterous stroke to approve the essentials of Bevin's policy, while arguing: "Mr. Bevin has managed to make British foreign policy equally disliked in France and Germany, by Jew and Arab, and by Communist and anti-Communist forces."

[22] *The Times,* Feb. 16 and 21, 1950.

[23] *The Times,* Feb. 18, 1950.

[24] *The Times,* Feb. 21, 1950.

[25] In reply to a questioner Bevin said: "Your suggestion is that if it is turned over to Mr. Churchill, he is greater than the lot of us and will be able to deal with it. I do not believe it." *The Times,* Feb. 17, 1950.

had to be very wary of offending any minority within the Parliamentary Labour Party. Apart from the defense program, the Government was subsequently very careful not to rouse any leftist suspicions about hostility to Communist China or about imperialism.

Unfortunately, all these developments conspired to paralyze the initiative of the British Government. The very real difficulties for Britain in associating with Western Europe were exaggerated to smother the breath of enterprise. Wesern Europe was alarmed.

b. FRENCH ANXIETY AND THE PROGRESS OF FUNCTIONAL UNION.

President Auriol voiced the growing anxiety of France in a speech to the British Parliament. For such a formal occasion he spoke more plainly than might have been expected. By emphasizing that "aggression cannot be discouraged by lining up a limited array of military resources" he expressed his dissatisfaction with the largely military British approach to Europe. Instead, he insisted that "it is our duty to hasten by every means and in every sphere with that close association war would inevitably produce, but which, if accomplished in good time, can in itself prevent war."[26]

In May, 1950, the N.A.T.O. Council of Foreign Ministers agreed to establish a permanent Council to which each government would send a deputy. Here some approach to functional union was achieved, for the agreed concept of national contributions "to achieve the necessary integrated strength for North Atlantic defense"[27] required military

---

[26] *New York Times,* March 10, 1950. Cf. Anne O'Hare McCormick's commentary on March 11.

[27] Bevin's address at a public session of the Conference, *The Daily Telegraph,* May 19, 1950.

123

preparations not in terms of national but of the overall needs of Western European defense. It was also agreed that "the problem of adequate military forces and the necessary financial costs should be examined as one and not as separate problems." The wider perspective of British policy, however, appeared in the agreement of the French and British Foreign Ministers to bring the United States and Canada into informal association with the representatives of the O.E.E.C.[28]

c. DEBATE ON THE SCHUMAN PLAN.

Britain was satisfied with this functional progress. France, confronted by Germany's advance to sovereignty, was not. A great weariness engulfed France, expressing itself in neutralism and in a fear that France, having lost all initiative, was being remorselessly driven to rearmament and war. Foreign Minister Schuman saw in this feeling a challenge and an opportunity. The opportunity involved the solution of three problems: the ending of Franco-German hostility; provisions for dealing with an anticipated surplus of steel; and the necessity of compelling Britain to take a clear stand on European Union. Drawing upon a multitude of earlier suggestions, he propounded the Schuman Plan, a proposal that the coal, iron and steel industries of Germany, France and Western Europe be placed under a supranational authority. The proposal was made without diplomatic preparation. "Almost in all questions we found ourselves up a blind alley. Above all we wanted to remove the terrible mortgage of the fear of war haunting us. We had to give a new zest to

---

[28] This was "a clear acceptance of the British view that it is more important to attach America and Canada however loosely, to the continent than it is to tie Western Europe into a neat parcel." *The Economist*, LVIII (May 27, 1950), 1158.

our will to peace and seek the possibility of a psychological shock to give this desire impetus. That is why the plan was made public. What determined us to act as we did was the conviction that we had to move quickly and that only France could usefully take the initiative."[29]

The gesture got a spectacular press. The British response, at first, was reserved and ultimately negative. But before a clear negative emerged, the British response had been handled with such professional clumsiness that the darkest suspicions about Britain were aroused and the Conservative Party was enabled to reap considerable partisan advantage.

Bevin's first response was that of noncommittal curiosity. He raised questions with Robert Schuman about the effect of the plan on living standards.[35] Thereafter, the British attitude grew more reserved, approaching the Foreign Office policy towards Aristide Briand's proposal of European Federal Union, "caution, though cordial caution." The same attitude was shared by Attlee. When the negotiations for British participation began, Attlee was vacationing in France, Cripps was in the Alps, Bevin was preparing for an operation and Herbert Morrison was in charge of the government. In these negotiations, the British and French did a fair job of caricaturing their national characters. For participation in the formulation of the Plan, the French insisted on an initial acceptance of the supranational authority. The pooling, they insisted, was a desirable thing, and the participating governments should instruct their experts to devise the means to achieve the end. The British reaction to

---

[29] Schuman's speech to the national congress of the M.R.P., *Daily Telegraph,* May 22, 1950.

[30] *The Observer,* May 14, 1950.

this was that they were being asked to buy a pig in a poke.[31] Indeed, it is quite likely that, while French insistence on accepting the principle of the Plan was well advised, it was also designed to keep the British out.[32]

The final British position, then, was a cordial caution which expressed the hope, that when the plan took shape, Britain would find it acceptable. Then came a bombshell, a magnificent demonstration of the fact that the left wing of the Labour Party did not know or care what its right wing was doing. The National Executive Committee of the Labour Party issued a pamphlet, "European Unity." This contained many points which even a Conservative manifesto would have accepted. Other parts were very doctrinaire and stressed the impossibility of joining capitalist and socialist economies. Labour's enemies at home and many Europeans

---

[31] The economist, Lionel Robbins, wrote in a letter to *The Times,* June 16, 1950: "Like the public in the days of the South Sea Bubble, we are being asked to subscribe without reserve to an undertaking the nature of which shall hereafter be revealed." Other British comments recalled the Latin beau geste of the Franco-Italian Customs Union, which, proclaimed as a desirable end, achieved very little in practice.

[32] See British White Paper, Cmd. 7970, "Anglo-French Discussion" (London, 1950), and William Diebold, Jr., "Imponderables of the Schuman Plan," *Foreign Affairs,* XXIX (Oct., 1950), 114-129. Lord Brand commented in the House of Lords: "I should say that the French were more concerned to maintain their principle of high authority in relation to Germany than to see the British taking part in the negotiations. They have the object, I am sure, of making the partnership with Germany very difficult to break." This is confirmed by Robert Schuman's comment on Soviet proposals for a German Peace treaty: "My policy is never to let Germany be free to act alone." *New York Times,* March 25, 1952. A negative attitude to the Schuman Plan appeared among many Labour supporters, for example, British members of the executive board of the International Confederation of Free Trade Unions and British members of the International Miners Union. *Christian Science Monitor,* June 7, 1950; *New York Times,* June 11, 1950. British trade unionists earlier had expressed similar reservations about the Jouhaux Plan. An international plan must not interfere with Britain's nationalization policy and with full employment.

promptly seized upon the points as the explanation of the Labour Government's unwillingness to participate in the Schuman Plan.[33]

For the Conservatives this was partisan manna from heaven, or, at any rate, a red herring from Transport House. At almost the same time, Bevin's Parliamentary Under-Secretary for Foreign Affairs, Ernest Davies, expounded the triumphs of British economic planning to the United Nations Economic Commission for Europe. In the field of economic cooperation, he said, "nothing can be done which would endanger that planning."[34] Prime Minister Attlee endured an uncomfortable ordeal in the Commons, while he sought to remain loyal to his Labour Party associates and at the same time to affirm his wishes for the success of the Schuman Plan. Later, the Conservatives made a great play of their willingness to diminish national sovereignty. Eden indicated that the Conservatives were willing to accept membership in a high authority—he did not say supranational—"provided we were satisfied as to the conditions and safe-

---

[33] "Socialists would of course welcome a European economic union which was based on international planning for full employment, social justice and stability. But international planning can only operate on the basis of national planning. And many European governments have not shown either the will or the ability to plan their own economies," "European Unity" (London, 1950), p. 7. The statement got a particularly bad press, for Hugh Dalton presented it to a press conference in an insufferably arrogant manner. This performance amply justified Attlee's decision in 1945 to substitute Bevin for Dalton as Foreign Secretary. Francis Williams, *Socialist Britain* (New York, 1949), pp. 55-57. Many European Socialists were shocked by the doctrinaire and nationalist harshness of "European Unity." The French Socialist, André Philip, wrote: "The doctrine of Socialism in one country, whose inevitable misdeeds in Russia were already denounced by Trotsky, becomes a total absurdity in the small nations of the West. Those who cling to it, with the laudable aim of protecting social gains, are brought by the force of things to take in foreign policy more and more conservative positions contrary to the socialist spirit and the democratic ideal." *New York Herald Tribune,* August 27, 1950.

[34] *New York Times,* June 11, 1950.

guards." Churchill, after pointedly referring to Bevin's illness, said that the French made the conditions difficult because they feared Labour's obstructionism. This was a daring thing to say, for Churchill himself later taunted Cripps for not being prepared to participate in the negotiations and to say no to the French. Anthony Eden said that the failure of the plan would be a political disaster, and its success, without Britain, would be full of dangers to Britain. This gave the game away. "I say deliberately that in all its dreams of wedge-driving Europe could hope for nothing better than the reduction of Britain to the status of observer in Franco-German relations." Churchill, again, expressed the British dilemma; "The question is whether British reluctance to assert herself within a movement towards European unity will not bring about just this very danger of a neutral geographical bloc, and whether we, by standing out, may not become responsible for bringing about the very situation the Socialist Executive in their pamphlet so rightly fear."[35] For the first time since the Labour victory in 1945, the Conserva-

---

[35] *Parliamentary Debates,* House of Commons, Vol. 476, clmns. 1915, 1918, 1925, 2144-2145, 2149, 2156, 2167. The Schuman Plan occasioned this revealing moment of truth about Britain and European Union. Mr. Churchill was expressing the British governess complex. "They wish Britain to participate in a negotiation in order that it may prevent the formation of a European union in which Britain could not participate." Walter Lippman in the *New York Herald Tribune,* July 6, 1950. The American commentator was referring to the views of the editor of *The Economist.* These were not far removed from Churchill's views. *The Times,* June 5, 1950, put the difficulty succinctly: "This country desires the closest possible association with its neighbors of the Continent, yet any Government—whether Labor or Conservative—are bound to envisage that association not in terms of a supranational body but first and foremost as an association of Governments freely working together and even agreeing to accept limitations on their separate actions or policies under the terms of an agreement negotiated together for a specific purpose. It is in that spirit that the Organization for European Economic Cooperation has worked out and that the military and political provisions of the Brussels Treaty and Atlantic Pact are being elaborated."

tives pressed for a parliamentary vote on a foreign policy question.[36]

The pamphlet made a stir in the United States. The British Ambassador, Sir Oliver Franks, felt impelled to write a letter to explain British policy to the Senate Foreign Relations Committee: "Britain is a power with world-wide interests, responsibilities and commitments . . . cooperation with her Western European neighbors and the vigorous promotion of unity in Europe is a vital necessity for Britain . . . it is only as the focus of the Commonwealth that the strength of Britain can make its full contribution to European recovery and unity." It is the aim of British policy to reconcile these relationships. This explanation gave Senator McCarran a final insight into the British position: "we cannot shut our eyes to the British position and if we find that the British government is committed to policies which prevent it from becoming a part of a united Europe, without reservation, we should cease to carry on a program based on the assumption that it will do so."[37]

Churchill's anger with Attlee appears to have been caused by the fact that Attlee's policy towards the Schuman Plan made Britain's position too clear. Eden and Churchill, both, made many suggestions which would have enabled the British Government to smother the plan with negatives. They, doubtless, proved that they would have been capable

---

[36] Although the Conservatives did not disagree with the principles of Labour's foreign policy, this division represented a protest against the ineptitude of Labour's methods. This Conservative position was expressed in a radio speech by Richard A. Butler: "We Conservatives feel that we could give a new lead. We would call our Commonwealth family together and work out with them a joint plan of action in matters of defence and trade. Then we would bring them together with Western Europe and the United States of America in a mighty union." *New York Times,* June 25, 1950.

[37] *New York Herald Tribune,* June 24, 1950.

of more finesse, but Attlee's position, being honest and definite, enabled the French to see the problem of German industries with greater precision.[38]

3. *Aggression in Korea and British Policy in the Far East.*

The British debate over the Schuman Plan took place just after the North Korean aggression began. This overt attack from a Soviet-dominated government gradually changed the emphasis of Britain from recovery to rearmament, and therewith removed the prospect of a steel surplus in Europe. It intensified American pressure for German participation in European defense. The devastation in Korea also reminded Europeans of their weakness and of the probable horrors of a new war to liberate a Soviet-controlled continent. Initially, however, the North Korean War highlighted the divergence of British and American policies in the Far East.

a. THE COLOMBO PLAN.

The United States, from the vantage point of a conquered and apparently docile Asiatic nation, Japan, looked out to China where war raged between a former ally, Chiang Kai-shek and Communist forces. Britain regarded Chiang less warmly, and viewed the Chinese struggle with the memory of recent experience gained in India and Indonesia.

---

[38] The Conservatives, who were at Strasbourg for a Council of Europe meeting, presented a counterproposal to the Schuman Plan. This proposal, which preserved the veto power for each state, was issued to the press, but was not raised in the Council of Europe's Assembly.- *New York Times,* August 9, 1950, and *Christian Science Monitor,* August 23, 1950. David Eccles, who failed to present the counterproposal, said: "The Schuman Plan was a test case for Great Britain." *Summary of the Debates in the Consultative Assembly of Europe,* Vol. I (London, 1951), clmn. 53.

The nationalism of large Asiatic countries could not be opposed, even if nationalism took the form of revolution.

Bevin had earlier indicated that Britain would seek to promote stability in Asia by fostering its economic development. Urged on by Australia, anxiously eager to harness Asian nationalism to friendship with the non-Communist world, Bevin and the Commonwealth Ministers (Colombo, Jan. 9-14, 1950) agreed to provide measures and machinery for promoting the economic development of Southeast Asia.[39] A similar meeting at Sydney and a later one in London completed the outlines of the Colombo Plan (Nov. 28, 1950). Limited resources and the magnitude of the problems caused the planners to think less in terms of increasing production immediately. Instead, long range measures of providing irrigation and electricity, and of increasing technical knowledge, were the principal targets. In short, the program, while barely enabling the area to maintain its position, would "fortify the economy of the area to provide a sound basis for improvement in the future."[40]

This Plan is a brave but not very substantial effort to strengthen Asia's economic development. There are many difficulties in the project. The ambitious goals of the Colombo Plan appear modest before the prospect of Asia's growing population. The poverty and instability of the area do not invite capital investment. Asian nationalism is suspicious of foreign aid and investment as new forms of imperialism and tutelage. Moreover, the desire of Asian nationalists to advance rapidly towards industrialism, as a symbol of strength and independence, runs counter to the necessity of first acquiring capital by exports of primary products and

---

[39] Executive decisions are not made at Commonwealth Conferences.
[40] *The Times*, Nov. 29, 1950.

raw materials.[41]

The Colombo Conference displayed the new British Commonwealth at its best. The Prime Minister of Ceylon presided over the sessions, which met in a former citadel of imperial power overlooking a parade ground of the British Army. To the Plan itself, Britain could offer little capital, apart from releases from the sterling balances. But Britain had put in a strong claim for being associated with the economic development of Asia, even though capital would have to come from other sources. Perhaps Britain hoped to essay the role of mediator between American assistance and Asiatic sensitivity.

The Conference, scheduled in 1948, coincided with the diplomatic negotiations between the triumphant Mao Tse-tung and the Soviet Union. It revealed a multitude of differences, even on such matters as Indo-China, where the regime of Bao Dai was eventually recognized by the British Government. India refused to recognize the genuineness of this French attempt to avoid Communism in meeting the demands of Asian nationalism. Immediately before the Conference Britain announced willingness to recognize Communist China.

For lack of anything else Britain, then, favored Asian nationalism, and, in seeking the collaboration of such states as India and Pakistan, had to listen to their views about the Chinese Revolution. Burma, it is true, had proved a bad bet and was torn by civil war. Communist guerillas had begun their costly campaign in Malaya. But serious British

---

[41] *Columbo Plan for the Cooperative Economic Development in South and South-East Asia: Report by the Commonwealth Consultative Committee* (Cmd. 8080, London, 1950). There is a good summary in *The Times*, Nov. 29, 1950. A brief and illuminating examination of the problems of development in economically backward areas appears in W. K. Hancock, *The Wealth of Colonies* (New York, 1950).

opinion had early been concerned by the apparent imminence of a Chinese Communist victory.[42] The cold war loomed
with tropic heat in Asia. Even the United Nations Economic
Commission for Asia and the Far East was checkmated by
bitter Soviet criticism of its development plans as weighted
in favor of the "Colonial Powers," the enemies of Eastern
freedom.[43]

b. BRITAIN AND CHINA.

In the tragic disintegration of the forces of Chiang Kai-
shek Britain played the role of spectator.[44] In 1948 she agreed
to facilitate the activities of the Chinese Customs Officers
in checking smuggling from Hong Kong. She also provided
a few ships for Nationalist use. But on June 8, 1949, British
policy was well summed up by A. V. Alexander, then Minister of Defense: British policy is "to create the friendliest
possible relationship with whatever may be at the given
moment the Government of China."[45] British Consular offic-

---

[42] "Mao-Tse-tung may conceivably develop into the Tito of the Far
East. But to count on that would be as foolish for the West as to refuse all
dealings with a Communist Government in Nanking. Faced with a completely
uncertain future, Western policy must be guided not by theories but by events,
while every effort is made to build up the prosperity of all available territories,
eastward from Malaya, to serve as strongholds against further Communist
advance." *The Observer*, December 19, 1948. *The Observer* was inclined to
regard the whole of Eastern and South East Asia as lost. It appeared to consider the retention of any British position there as a minor miracle.

[43] *The Observer*, December 12, 1948.

[44] "We have explained to the Chinese Government, whose positions we
understand, that our financial and economic position precluded us from doing
anything very material for China. However, . . . we can not be indifferent to
the fate of either our nationals or our extensive trading interests in China."
Bevin, *Weekly Hansard*, House of Commons, No. 109, December 9, 1948,
clmns. 568-569.

[45] *South China Morning Post*, June 9, 1949, quoted in A. S. B. Olver
"Outline of British Policy in East and Southeast Asia, 1945-May 1950"
mimeographed paper (London, 1950), p. 18. Alexander's mission was to in-

133

ials remained at their posts when the Communists occupied their areas.[46] When the Chinese Foreign Minister on January 8, 1949, asked the American, British, French and Soviet Governments to act as intermediaries in beginning negotiations with the Chinese Communists, the United States[47] replied that in view of the failure of earlier efforts, American mediation then could serve no useful purpose. The British declined on the ground that British participation would be contrary to the Moscow declaration and would only confuse the issue.

Faced with Communist victory the British did not engage in a great debate, for Britain was not deeply concerned with the China Sea area. She was prepared to urge on the United States the necessity of bolstering "non-Communist Asia, which the fall of China puts into mortal danger."[48] Britain could argue that European recovery and military defense were jeopardized by Southeast Asia's struggle against European colonialism in Indonesia and Indo-China.

British commercial interests in the Far East began pressing for diplomatic recognition of Mao's government. Britain protested against the Nationalist air blockade of Chinese ports. When Dr. Tsiang (November 3, 1949) submitted to the Political Committee of the U.N. General Assembly a draft resolution calling for non-recognition of the Communist regime, Britain supported one that maintained an open

---

volve the traditional maneuver of expressing Britain's alertness and concern about Communist intentions towards Hong-Kong and to express some good will. Before his visit, orders to strengthen British garrisons at Hong Kong had been issued. Alexander said much the same thing in London, June 14, 1949.

[46] Prime Minister Attlee, *Weekly Hansard,* House of Commons, No. 124, April 26, 1949, clmns. 25-26.

[47] *United States Relations with China* (Washington, 1949), pp. 290-291.

[48] *The Observer,* February 6, 1949; *The Times,* March 1, 1949, sounded a similar note, though it recognized that Burma, also, was an object lesson.

door policy. Sir Terence Shone argued that recognition should be decided by the facts and not by dislike of the Communist government.[49] Bevin had doubtless discussed recognition with Acheson in Sept., 1949, when the possibility of a new approach for the conclusion of a Japanese peace treaty was raised. On November 16, 1949, Bevin said that the government had not, as yet, come to a decision: "there are a lot of issues involved — the United Nations, the Security Council, and the question of the views of the United States and our own Commonwealth. In a great changeover of this character, one has to act with caution, reasonable speed and with an idea of producing the best results."[50] The last point suggests that the recognition was only a matter of timing.

At Singapore, in the first week of November, 1949, a meeting of British diplomats and military officials, concerned with the Far East and South East Asia, unanimously recommended the recognition of Communist China.[51] The British position was that recognition would at least permit the British Government to discuss the protection of British interests in China. Recognition would, also, increase Mao's contacts with the West. Further, although the United States Government was not prepared to follow the British action, it may not have been wholly opposed to the attempt.

Recognition produced no immediate results, apart from proclaiming the fact that Britain was not implacably hostile to a Communist China. Prime Minister Nehru was presumably satisfied, but British commercial interests in China experienced no benefits. The Chinese Communist Government unhurriedly raised questions and conditions for the es-

---

[49] *The Times,* December 5, 1949.
[50] *Weekly Hansard,* House of Commons, No. 141, November 16, 1949, clmn. 2017.
[51] "Unanimity" was stressed by *The Times,* January 7, 1950.

tablishment of full diplomatic relations. Meanwhile, Britain's recognition caused a greater rift in the Anglo-American approach to Asia. This rift hardened when the United States took the initiative in resistance to the North Korean aggression.

c. BRITAIN AND THE UNITED NATIONS' ACTION IN KOREA.

The British Government supported the United States in proposing United Nations' resistance to the North Korean aggression. American espousal of collective security was reassuring, but Britain was painfully conscious of the limited military resources available for such action. Apart from naval forces, the British Government was reluctant to provide ground troops, for the campaign in Malaya and the armed posture of Hong Kong drew heavily on the available infantry. An even more serious occasion for British reluctance arose from a fear about the scope of the commitment in Korea. Would Korea become another interminable Greece, Indo-China or Malaya? More specifically, Britain feared complications with Communist China, whom she had recognized.

The multiplicity of Britain's relations with the Commonwealth, Europe and the United States gave British policy in the succeeding months the appearance of drift and opportunism. In the days of triumphant United Nations' advance, the British Minister of State, Kenneth Younger, submitted to the Political Committee of the United Nations General Assembly a resolution which recommended general measures, including elections, for the establishment of "a unified, independent and democratic Government in the Sovereign State of Korea.[52] This resolution, taken in days of military success, served as General MacArthur's

---

[52] This was adopted on Oct. 7, 1950.

justification for crossing the 38th Parallel.[53]

After China's forces joined the fighting and the United Nations troops were driven back, the British Government in some chagrin returned to its original caution. Even as the United Nations' forces approached the Yalu River, the British Government was becoming uneasy. On November 29, Bevin declared that for some weeks he had been working on a proposal to draw a line across the Korean Peninsula to stabilize the fighting front there. Bevin firmly added that the British Government would not recognize Syngman Rhee's authority north of the Thirty-Eighth parallel.[54] This speech was peculiarly unsatisfactory, for it dealt with plans for the reconstruction of Korea and with might-have-beens. It hardly responded to the gravity of the situation in Korea, and its inadequacy enabled Churchill again to rise to the dignity of the tragedy.

---

[53] Bevin, addressing the Labour Party Conference at Margate, defended the United States against charges of aggression, acclaimed American intervention in Korea as a precedent which should cause aggressors to think twice before they acted. The unification and rehabilitation of Korea would be another great precedent. *The New York Times*, Oct. 6, 1950. A month earlier, on his arrival in New York, Bevin was more cautious. He refused to believe that China was wholly gone. He declined to evaluate the strategic importance of Formosa, but warned against overemphasis on strategy. The future of China "will depend upon the approach. . . . Asia should be looked on as Asia," without singling out its parts. Bevin considered it as an area emerging from years of foreign occupation with a newly developing "nationalistic conscience." Britain had won the friendship of India by granting independence, and, by implication, the United States could gain the friendship of China by recognizing Mao Tse-tung. *The New York Times*, Sept. 13, 1950.

[54] House of Commons, November 29, 1950; Lord Salisbury proposed the defensive line on November 15, 1950; Eden and Churchill seconded the proposal. Churchill's speech on November 30, 1950, gave a masterly survey of world affairs. Of the Korean war he said: "Surely, however, the United Nations should avoid by every means in their power becoming entangled inextricably in a war with China. . . . The sooner the Far Eastern diversion— because vast as it is, it is but a diversion—can be brought into something like a static condition, and stabilization is effected, the better it will be for all the purposes which the United Nations have in hand. For it is in Europe that the world cause will be decided."

Mr. Bevin was restrained, possibly he wished to give an example of calmness. The latter quality was notably absent, even in Britain, by the end of the foreign affairs debate. British alarm took the characteristic form of extreme concern over possible American rashness. This had been a constant theme of Labour's left-wing.[55] The defeat of General MacArthur's forces and the violent expressions of American opinion roused a British demand that the case for caution and prudence be pressed by the British Government. A misinterpretation of President Truman's remark about the use of the atom bomb brought the anxiety to a climax. Prime Minister Attlee then announced that he was about to confer with President Truman, to attempt to renew between the political leaders of the two states that friendly understanding which Roosevelt and Churchill had achieved. Mr. Attlee's mission was to resolve the dilemma arising from the fact that Britain and the United States were firmly bound in a military alliance in Europe and followed divergent policies in Asia.[56]

---

[55] Tom Driberg, Labour M.P., urged the United States to "keep your heads and keep the war small." *New York Times,* July 5, 1950.

[56] Conservatives and Labourites were agreed in regarding a war against China as wholly undesirable. Labour members of Parliament had been urging a mission to Washington, and Conservatives agreed. *The Economist* was somewhat smug in its exaggeration of the calmness of the British debate: "Members witnessed a spectacle not seen in many years, the development and execution of new policy as the debate progressed. Mr. Bevin's calm but unenterprising speech laid the first foundations upon which Mr. Eden, Mr. Churchill, and Mr. Butler successively built until Mr. Attlee's announcement of his decision to fly to Washington appeared to emerge more as the result of a joint decision from inter-party conference than as the personal action of the head of the Government." *The Economist,* CLIX (Dec. 9, 1950), 988. Another comment reveals more clearly the decided lack of calm in the House of Commons. "In the elation about Mr. Attlee's announcement that he was flying to Washington there was just a touch of the false relief with which the House of 1938 received Mr. Chamberlain's announcement that he was flying to Munich." *The Observer,* Dec. 3, 1950. Mr. Bevin's failure to accompany Attlee underscored his physical incapacity for the post he held.

The confusion and excitement were understandable, for the situation was unprecedented. An apparently triumphant vindication of collective security had been defeated by the incursion of troops from another state. Officially, in the topsy-turvy world created by totalitarian diplomacy, these troops were volunteers, official volunteers of totalitarian China. Principle and logic demanded that China be branded as the enemy. But American leaders, also balked at the consequences of this logic. Mr. Attlee's mission involved a preaching to the converted. President Truman and Dean Acheson were in accord with the British opinion that it was "not a question of Britain forcing her policy on America, but of reason and reality forcing an unwelcome policy on both of us."[57] For the moment, however, policy could not be enunciated in detail until the momentum of fighting had slowed down and had allowed the new fog of war to clear.

Although there were many matters to discuss, Mr. Attlee's visit created embarrassment for Truman and Acheson. The Prime Minister vigorously repudiated any intention to appease. His coming, however, complicated a difficult situation, and increased the suspicions of domestic critics of American foreign policy.[58] Continued Chinese intervention subsequently caused Britain to yield to further American pressure, but the divergence of policies persisted. Britain was committed to the consequences of recognizing Communist China. She shared, as the British Minister of State, Kenneth Younger said, the Indian view that China would not indefinitely remain "a tool of Soviet policy."[59] The

[57] *The Observer,* Dec. 3, 1950.

[58] Attlee and his advisers successfully avoided the numerous hazards which British diplomats encounter in the United States. American news photographers waited in readiness to snap any one of Attlee's advisers who carried an umbrella. *Christian Science Monitor,* Dec. 18, 1950.

[59] Nehru had not risen to the level of events, when he described the

Asians must determine the fate of Asia, and the objective of Anglo-American diplomacy must be "to rally to our side the maximum amount of Asian support by helping them realize both their nationalist and social objectives, free from the domination of Soviet imperialism." Indeed, by implication, Mr. Younger urged the United States to follow Britain's example and policy, for "my country has been quick to grasp the mood of the new era" in Asia.[60]

Meanwhile, a British career diplomat, Sir Gladwyn Jebb, delegate to the Security Council, skillfully adjusted himself to the glare of United Nations' diplomacy. His defense of American and United Nations' policy on television broadcasts of Security Council sessions did not convince or notably mollify the Soviet Union, but did increase the friendly feeling of eastern Americans for Britain.

4. *European Union and Mr. Churchill.*

United States' leadership in resisting the North Korean aggression heartened many Europeans and yet roused other fears. The defense ministers of the Brussels Treaty met at Fontainebleau and "recognized the necessity of accelerating without delay the production of war materials and of increasing the defensive power of the land, sea and air forces as a guarantee against any aggression."[61] Apart from the costs of rearmament, two other fears troubled European leaders. The French were determined to have closer co-ordination of defense programs. As the French Minister of Defense put it, France would make a maximum effort if

---

participation of some nations in the United Nations' action in Korea as "showing off." *New York Times,* July 8, 1950.

[60] Speech to the Foreign Policy Association, *New York Times,* Dec. 3, 1950.

[61] *New York Herald Tribune,* July 21, 1950.

Britain and the United States made a similar effort in Europe. "There should be no question about having a French infantry, a British navy and an American air force."[62] The other fear was the possibility of German rearmament.

In this fear Churchill saw a chance to take the initiative in encouraging European Union as a means of using German military resources. Moreover, his initiative might have been intended to forestall the desire of many Europeans who were prepared to federate without Britain.[63] The dexterity and imagination of Churchill in the Strasbourg sounding board embarrassed the British government by efficiently disclosing its torpidity. It was the perfect place for a grand gesture and Churchill rose to the occasion. Paul Reynaud prepared the way by remarking (August 9) that "a European Minister for War must at last be found, and they need not look outside the gathering to find him."[64] Two days later the proposed European Minister for War, Churchill, moved a resolution "for the immediate creation of a unified European Army subject to proper European democratic control and acting in full cooperation with the United States and Canada."[65]

The gesture was magnificent, and immediately support for a European Army was widely expressed. It stirred Eu-

---

[62] French delegates to the North Atlantic Council of Deputies believed "that the dangers to Atlantic planning from proceeding from national programs have been more than fully demonstrated by the difficulties of the O.E.E.C. in preparing for the management and utilization of the Marshall Plan aid." *New York Times,* August 4, 1950.

[63] *New York Times,* August 23, 1950.

[64] *Summary of the Debates in the Consultative Assembly of the Council of Europe,* Vol. I, clmn. 36.

[65] Churchill justified this action by noting that the Committee of Ministers had invited the Assembly to approve the United Nations' action in Korea. Thus, according to Churchill, the Ministers "had virtually invited them to consider the military position of Western Europe." *Ibid.,* I, clmns. 59-61.

ropeans with a sense of dynamism and purpose. Churchill could express Europe's fears that a Russian initiative in Europe would mean a Russian victory and that "the systematic liquidation of all elements hostile to Communism would leave little which could be recognized by the rescuers or the survivors."[66]

These fears were the best arguments to close "the gap in European defenses" as "the surest means of preventing a third world war."[67] He further reassured the fearful that the mere closing of the gap could not in itself be provocative to Russia. Even Labour delegates to the Assembly admitted that the pressure of events made it impossible to oppose Churchill's motion.[68] But what did it mean? It is unlikely that, even at the time, Mr. Churchill expected Britain to join in a European Army. Churchill, like Bevin looked to the wider resources of the Atlantic Community.[69] If he had been in power, Mr. Churchill could not have made such a proposal. But at Strasbourg he could do so, and so call atten-

---

[66] *Christian Science Monitor,* August 12, 1950.

[67] *Summary of the Debates in the Consultative Assembly of the Council of Europe,* I, clmn. 60.

[68] M. Edelman, "The Council of Europe, 1950," *International Affairs,* XXVII (1951), 29-30. "In spite of this brave reception, it is a little difficult to discover precisely what Mr. Churchill and his supporters have in mind." *The Economist,* CLIX (Aug. 19, 1950), 345.

[69] See negative remarks by Bevin in *New York Times,* Sept. 13, 1950. Speaking to the Labour Conference at Margate he indicated that he had no faith in a European army. After two wars Europe was weak, and strength had to be sought in the Atlantic Community. *New York Times,* Oct. 6, 1950. After Pleven proposed a European Army, Bevin replied on Nov. 29, 1950, that it was "not the present policy of His Majesty's Government to contribute United Kingdom forces to a European Army." Churchill, upon becoming Prime Minister, repeated Bevin's position in a more positive fashion: "We do not propose to merge in the European Army but we are already joined to it. Our troops are on the spot and we shall do our utmost to make a worthy and effective contribution to the deterrents against aggression. . . . There is the N.A.T.O. Army. Inside the N.A.T.O. Army there is the European Army and inside the European Army there is the German Army."

tion to the necessity of closing the gap in European defenses.

French efforts to give substantial detail to the proposal proved unacceptable to the Germans and were generally viewed as impractical. The smaller nations, especially the Netherlands, were full of misgivings about this Napoleonic army. On this issue, once again, the European nations used British unwillingness as an excuse for their own reluctance to unify Europe. Ultimately, though not with finality as it turned out, the Defense and Military Committees of the N.A.T.O. approved a plan to add German "regimental combat teams" to the defense of Western Europe. At the Brussels meeting of the North Atlantic Treaty Organization, December 18-19, 1950, the establishment of an integrated force under a centralized command was approved. General Eisenhower was to be given comand of this force. This, not the German agreement, was decisive. If the United States activly participated in preparations for the defense of Europe, there was, at least, a chance that German military resources would be available for the defense of Germany and of Europe. But this reversal of Potsdam had yet to reckon with the fears of Europe upon which the Soviet Union had intensified its threats.

CHAPTER SIX

The Continuing Ordeal:
The Last Year of the Labour Government

> *"Russia must be attacked from Asia, troops should be sent to the Persian Gulf, and the Empress of India should order her armies to clear Central Asia of the Muscovites, and drive them into the Caspian."*
>
> Disraeli (1876)

> *"But the ministers, as I say, go to the housetops to proclaim to every bazaar in the East that they do not know what to do, and that, after all this anxiety, they are going to scuttle out of the country as fast as they can. What I want your Lordships chiefly to observe is the consequence of such conduct, which is of the most destructive and deleterious kind. It may have been our policy to quit Afghanistan, but if we quit it in this spirit and after such declarations every military adventurer feels, "This is my opportunity: the British are going to leave this country, and I will succeed them as far as I can." Clearly, you have produced a state of anarchy, and at last you say that you will consummate your confession of impotence and blundering by giving up the city of Candahar."*
>
> Disraeli

The Labour Government's last year in office was turbulent, and was marked by divisions within the Party. The Labour Party was defeated in the October election amidst a confusing debate on the loss of Iran, Egypt's determination to annul the treaty of 1936, and on charges of Tory warmongering. This was characteristic of the whole year, for foreign policy had such important repercussions on the life of Britons at home that foreign policy did intrude in the domestic political struggle to an unusual extent. With rare historical precision, humiliation and defeat pursued the Labour Government to the day of polling. After the year's ordeal the Labour leaders, probably, felt a momentary relief when they were free of the burdens of office and of the responsibility for meeting a new financial crisis, in part the result of Britain's armaments effort. But, though the record of the Labour Government ended in several failures, failure was not writ large over its whole record. The voters were sufficiently satisfied or loyal to give the Labour Party a plurality of the popular vote, but not control of Parliament. Finally, the Conservatives, while charging Labour's foreign policy with incompetent implementation, approved the main lines of that policy.[1] Foreign affairs was not the *forte* of the Labour Party, but on the whole it had sturdily accepted the difficult task of defending the global interests of a trading island-empire in a world overshadowed by two continental super-powers.

1. *Britain and the United Nations: the Dilemma of Collective Security.*

In British opinion, one of these super-powers, the Soviet Union, appeared to be ready to expand wherever it could do so without the threat of general war. In other words, the Soviet Union did not plan war immediately or directly. It committed aggression by proxy, and might continue to do so, and it disposed of a world-wide army of

---

[1] On several occasions Mr. Churchill has paid to the Labour leader the not inconsiderable compliment of having adopted his proposals: "The policy which I outlined at Fulton five years ago has since been effectively adopted both by the United States and by the Socialist Party. Two years later by the Brussels Pact and in the following year by the North Atlantic Treaty, the whole substance and purpose of what I said was adopted and enforced by the Socialist Government, and today we all respect the foresight and wise courage of the late Ernest Bevin in helping to bring those great changes about." *Weekly Hansard,* Feb. 27, 1952.

propagandists and possible saboteurs. There were dangers of general war in the Soviet policy, but these arose more from hasty and ill-considered counterstrokes against Soviet expansionism. Herbert Morrison, before becoming Foreign Secretary, gave a Socialist twist to Britain's foreign policy: "Our job as Socialists in Britain is to do our best to make the Soviet rulers change their mind and until they change their mind we must take the necessary measures to protect ourselves. . . . We are spending these enormous sums on armaments not so as to fight a war with Russia, but so as to avoid the need to fight a war with Russia."[2]

Soviet expansionism, it was argued, was facilitated by colonial and Asiatic nationalism. Britain, however, had either allied with these forces, or was attempting to come to terms with them.

In the face of so formidable a threat to the scattered British possessions, Britain's course was obvious. It accepted and supported the other superpower's policy, the creation of situations of strength. Yet it did so with considerable initial and final misgivings about the United Nations' action in Korea. Failure of the United States to resist aggression in Korea would have envenomed the bitter debate about American foreign policy, and would have greatly strengthened European neutralism. Nevertheless, the British Government was fearful of the extensive obligations of collective security.

Britain's self-assigned course, therefore, was to contribute to the building of western strength, while fixing American attention to the main theatre of Western Europe. Not balancing of power but balanced and realistic thinking would be the British role. On one occasion, Bevin's successor, Herbert Morrison, mistaking the role for actual policy said that Britain had opposed the crossing of the 38th Parallel in Ko-

---

[2]   *The Observer,* March 4, 1951.

rea. But in the lighthearted days of apparent victory in Korea, the British do not appear to have made such a suggestion.[3]

The British Government prized the United Nations as an international meeting place. There, at any rate, the rest of the world could meet and argue with the Iron Curtain set. Sir Gladwyn Jebb said of the United Nations that, in spite of all "the recent despair and criticism of that body, it is just about as well suited for its primary purpose [to insure peace] as anything could be in the present condition of mankind." He went on to say that the fluctuations of public opinion between regarding the United Nations as the one hope of the world and describing it as a useless hypocrisy present "the chief danger which the United Nations has to face."[4]

a. THE CONDEMNATION OF CHINA.

When the presence of Chinese troops in Korea was first reported to the Security Council, Sir Gladwyn Jebb promptly proposed that the Chinese Communist Government be asked to participate in the discussions of MacArthur's re-

---

[3] General MacArthur, who can be a great literalist, denied that such a suggestion had been made. "If they did, it never reached me, and I had an Air Vice Marshall assigned to me as a special liaison officer from the British Government. I saw him at frequent intervals and nothing of the sort was ever communicated." *The Observer*, May 6, 1951.

[4] Speech to the New York City Bar Association, May 15, 1951; Text supplied by the British Information Services. Sir Gladwyn expressed some doubts about the "New Diplomacy" of the United Nations. "The ominous finger of the microphone, the hum of the recording machine in which every word is noted for the benefit of posterity, the insistent glare of the television lights, do indeed tend to produce a situation in which all diplomats or statesmen have to exercise a maximum caution and in which it is very difficult to negotiate in the old-fashioned sense of the word. . . . If we believe in democracy, therefore, we cannot say that the modern techniques are wrong. On the contrary, fundamentally they must be right."

port. Thereafter, Jebb played a skillful moderating role[5] until the United States had to be satisfied with a simple condemnation of China for having engaged in aggression in Korea. The American request for sanctions, which was opposed by the British and rejected, served to give substance to a general suspicion that the United States was intent on widening the War. Doubtless, this request was related to possibly necessary action in the still serious military situation in Korea. But the complex tides of American policy and opinion were not generally appreciated.

The condemnation of Red China as an aggressor finally allowed Britain to come closer to the United States on Formosa and on the shipment of war materials to China. While expressing no approval of Chiang Kai-shek, the British Government could argue that the implementation of the Cairo Declaration must be preceded by a settlement in Korea. In 1950 the British Government embargoed oil shipments to China, and continued to add to the list of forbidden goods. Thus, on May 14, 1951, Jebb indicated that the United Nations' resolution to stop the sending of war materials to China merely ratified existing British practice. Britain was opposed to any total embargo, for that merely would cut all ties between China and the non-Soviet world.[6]

Even here, Britain contrived to give this approach to the American position a reluctant appearance.[7] The failure of the Chinese to accept a cease-fire or negotiations, had nullified the British delaying action in the United Nations, and

---

[5] Warren Austin gave Jacob Malik the opportunity for an effective reply when the American delegate said that the Peiping representative should be "summoned."

[6] Labour's Secretary for War, John Strachey, approved the selective embargo, but insisted that a total embargo could only too easily be followed by more warlike measures. *The Observer*, May 20, 1951.

[7] When the General Assembly (Feb. 1, 1951) approved the much amended United States' resolution condemning China, Jebb opposed any

had, likewise, made their diplomatic recognition of China ineffective. As for the Korean fighting the British Government was now prepared to regard it as a police action and not a vindication of collective security. Chinese intervention had so changed the circumstances that, in effect, the British Government regarded the resolution on the unification of Korea as obsolete.[8]

2. The Atlantic Community and European Defense.

Britain's main hope of defense was in the N.A.T.O., especially in Britain's association with the United States. General Eisenhower as Supreme Commander of the N.A.T.O. army was enthusiastically acceptable to the British, not only as a man but even more as the most visible evidence of America's commitment to European defense. This dependence on the United States manifested the weakness of Britain's power position, and the truly great degree to which it had lost the mobility and diversity of approaches made possible by sea-power in the days of British dominance. Although Britain attempted to maintain its world-wide positions, its chief defensive necessity was the presence of a large army on the European continent. If the Continent falls, it is difficult to believe that the British island will remain defensible for any long period. But the diversity of British positions and its relatively small population make it impossible for Britain to commit a large army to the continent. In the event of war, the supplies to Britain and Europe will be

immediate consideration of sanctions: "Now that we have established our moral position by condemning the Central People's Government for engaging in aggression, the most important thing as we see it, is to concentrate on the problem of a peaceful settlement—or, as I would prefer to say, on an agreed solution—of the Korean question, rather than on the question of potential sanctions." *The Times,* Feb. 2, 1951.

8 *New York Times,* March 30, 1951. On Feb. 12, Mr. Attlee told the House of Commons that full U.N. consultation should precede any new cross-

carried from American waters to Britain, and a large part of the convoy duty will fall to the American navy.

a. CONTROVERSY OVER THE ATLANTIC COMMAND.

Such considerations apparently prompted Defence Minister Emmanuel Shinwell and the deputies of N.A.T.O. to agree to an American commander of the Atlantic area. Oddly enough, Attlee in announcing the arrangement appeared to be unaware of the domestic political disadvantage which this agreement would involve. In sheer terms of power and quotas the concession may have been justified. But this revelation of Britannia ruling the waves through the courtesy of an ally was a shock to British public opinion. Churchill instantly saw the advantage, and challenged Attlee in the House of Commons. The appearance of Churchill denouncing a Labour Government's concession to the United States had its amusing side. He, after all, was the trumpeter of Anglo-American fraternity, and he had often belabored Socialist mistrust and ingratitude towards the United States. His challenge of the American appointment served two purposes; it provided an opportunity to appeal to British national feeling against the Labour Government, and it gave an additional demonstration of the incompetence of Labour's handling of foreign affairs, for Britain had little enough bargaining power and, here, the Labour Government had squandered a tremendous chance for bargaining.[9]

---

ing of the 38th parallel. The Minister of State, Kenneth Younger, on March 22, 1951, amended this to the necessity of consultation before any general advance into North Korea. On April 11, Herbert Morrison summarized the British position "resistance to aggression, a free, independent, and unified Korea, and no extension of the conflict."

[9] The debate reveals the decided limits of the functional approach to union. It could, of course, be argued that the Atlantic Commander should have been selected by merit rather than by nationality. The more serious English papers did not find Attlee's concession so alarming. *The Times, The*

Following this tactical blunder, Prime Minister Attlee, who had again been performing Bevin's duties, finally determined on a reshuffling of the Cabinet. The ailing Bevin became Lord Privy Seal, and was succeeded as Foreign Secretary by Herbert Morrison. This selection may have been inevitable in terms of the conflicts within the Labour Party, but it was an unfortunate one. Morrison, the proponent of consolidation of Labour's gains against Aneurin Bevan's demand for a renewed march to Socialism, was preoccupied with Labour's electoral strategy and the preparations for the Festival of Britain. He had neither time nor inclination for careful study of foreign policy. Bevin had no deputy in any true sense. The long months of Bevin's illnesses and absence required of the new Foreign Secretary industry and application which he was unable to give. His very training as Party strategist encouraged him to take short-range views and to be ingenious without reference to overall ends. The fact that Mr. Attlee could find no one else of sufficient stature to replace Mr. Bevin reveals the failure of the Labour Party to develop younger leaders.

b. GERMANY'S CONTRIBUTION AND THE WRAITH
OF POTSDAM.

The interplay of Britain's foreign and domestic politics continued during the year. The upshot of this furore over

---

Observer and *The Economist,* were, if anything, a little disturbed by Churchill's pressing of an issue based on pride rather than reality. But they all recognized the partisan effectiveness of the Conservative leader's attack, for the issue was a very touchy one. *The Observer* commented under the heading "Back to Marlborough." "In any foreseeable world war, Britain will inevitably be concerned with her own defence, which means the defence on land of West Europe and the confined waters of the North Sea and Channel. . . . Because our whole history till now has been based on sea-power, it is hard for us to realize that in the context of a future war Britain will be primarily a land power." *The Observer,* Feb. 25, 1951. Thus, the public dispute was "unfortunate and

the Atlantic Command was to delay further action on it for several months and to obstruct a solution of the more difficult Mediterranean problem. The care of the Atlantic community's defense in Europe was in the hands of General Eisenhower. Even here, the objective, strength against a Russian attack, called for measures which to many Europeans, especially the French, were almost as objectionable as the prospect of Russian domination. But Western Europe could not be seriously defended without German participation. This had been recognized at the Brussels meeting of N.A.-T.O. in December. The form and number of German forces remained to be considered. As a result of Eisenhower's initial tour of investigation, the German issue was wisely postponed for a few months until arrangements about the other western powers had been concluded.

On this issue of supplying land forces in Europe, Britain presented difficulties. Forces were needed to defend the British island, for technically it was possible for the Soviet Union to attack Britain with rockets and aircraft from Eastern Germany.[10] The British Government refused to provide forces for the European army, envisaged by the Pleven Plan, and sent only an observer to the Paris meeting on the Plan.[11] This refusal encouraged the Belgians and Dutch to express their reluctance to commit themselves. Dirk Stikker, the Dutch Foreign Minister, said that he did not believe in a European federation without Britain, for the Netherlands was closer to the sterling area than to the Continent with its protectionism. While this British refusal was understand-

unnecessary." One reader promptly condemned the editor for going against the traditions of the last one thousand years, and expressed his determination to banish the paper from his household forever. *The Observer,* March 4, 1951.

[10] "The Defence of Britain," *The Economist,* CLX (March 31, 1951), 723-724.

[11] British reply (Jan. 31, 1951) to French invitation.

able in terms of Britain's preference for the Atlantic Pact, it impaired the European contribution to the Atlantic Pact's strength. The Brussels Pact appeared to have become meaningless, even though the tenth meeting of its Consultative Council in Brussels (Dec. 20, 1950) reaffirmed the obligations of its members. The same meeting agreed that a reorganization of the Western Union Defense organization was necessary. Bevin, holding on to the shreds of functionalism, joined with the other members in urging the continuation of political, social and cultural collaboration. But Western Union defensive power required a German contribution for any effectiveness.

Britain became reluctant to promote the immediate settlement of German armaments, apparently because it was troubled by the almost inflationary swelling of German bargaining power. The British High Commissioner argued: "If you bargain with the Germans on rearmament, you do not offer them partnership. We must make a different mental approach. . . . Germans, of all European nations, are the most difficult of partners, since they have not had much experience of partnership."[12] This British position appeared to be an argument for a speedy conclusion of agreement with Germany. But at the end of March the British High Commissioner in Germany refused to agree to the publication of a statement of principles for the treatment of Germany. This statement, accepted earlier by Kirkpatrick, was to be the preliminary to Germany's own initiation of rearmament. In this action, the British may have been simply seeking to delay the German action or to study the implications of the Schuman Plan in reference to the International Ruhr Authority. But the reason given was that the British did not

---

[12] Different excerpts from this speech are given in the *New York Times* and the *New York Herald Tribune,* Jan. 31, 1951.

wish to take further decisive steps until after the projected meeting of the Council of Foreign Ministers.[13]

This surprising recurrence of the theme of Big Power Unity may also have been prompted by domestic political considerations of the Labour Party. From November 3, 1950, the Soviet Union had been seeking a Four-Power meeting on the issue of the rearmament of Germany. Soviet objectives in calling the conference were to delay the incorporation of Germany into the Atlantic defense community, to play on the divisions within that community and to serve Communist peace propaganda by making the Atlantic powers appear to be intransigent. On March 5, 1951, the Deputies of the Foreign Ministers met in Paris to prepare an agenda for the meeting of the Foreign Ministers. Herbert Morrison, the British Foreign Secretary, was willing to hazard such a ministerial meeting, and none of the Powers involved dared to risk a direct refusal to meet. This extraordinary Conference, which had seventy-four meetings, apart from the usual informal sessions, largely became a wearisome effort to brand the Soviet Union or the Atlantic Pact Powers with responsibility for the failure to hold a conference of the Foreign Ministers. The Western Deputies outdid themselves in proposals for a Conference, but the fruitless meetings ended on June 21.[14] In the meantime, German rearmament arrangements were necessarily delayed.

c. THE STRAINS OF REARMAMENT.

Britain's proposed contribution to the strength of the Atlantic Community was revised upward in 1950. On Sep-

---

[13] Joseph Alsop in *New York Herald Tribune*, April 2, 1951.

[14] The main outlines of this interminable conference, a worthy successor to the Austrian Peace Treaty Negotiations and an ominous predecessor to the Korean Truce negotiations, are well described in S. T. Bindoff, "Four Deputies in Search of an Agenda," *World Affairs* (July, 1951), 263-273.

tember 12, 1950, Prime Minister Attlee announced a defense program which would amount to a total of £3,600,-000,000 for the years 1951-54. Later, on Jan. 29, 1951, in the face of American pressure and promises of aid, the Labour Government increased the total to £4,700,000,000. The British armed forces numbered 692,400 in mid-1950, and by March, 1951, the total had reached 934,600 (including, however, Reserve and Auxiliary Forces).[15] The aim for 1951-52 was ten Regular Army divisions and twelve Territorial divisions. As these were to be scattered throughout the Empire and in Germany, the total was not impressive. This fact, added to the Government's piecemeal approach to rearmament, caused Churchill to extend his challenge of the Labour Government's competence to the sphere of defense. This censure[16] in the armament debate of February 14 and 15, 1951, had some interesting repercussions in domestic alignments on foreign politics. First of all, the vote of censure momentarily united the Labour Party, sections of which had become critical of the Government's attitude to China in the United Nations.

Aneurin Bevan, speaking for the Government, called social democracy the most revolutionary movement of our time. Then, in an attempt to brand the Conservative motion as partisan, he said that not the Soviet but time, impatience for office, was Mr. Churchill's enemy. To this, Churchill nodded assent. Thus, Churchill's own motion for a moment covered over Labour's divisions, which Churchill considered responsible for the lack of coherent and sustained planning in defense. Labour's angry reaction to the

---

[15] *Britain's Defence Effort* (British Information Services, New York, 1951), p. 17.
[16] This censure of Labour's "ineptitude" recalled Labour's pre-war refusal to support Mr. Chamberlain's conscription proposal because Labour did not trust his foreign policy.

censure led to a new party slogan, which was used with some success in the October elections. Labour, so the line went, supported armaments for peace, whereas the Conservatives wanted armaments for war.

But the domestic difficulties of an armaments program, added to a fully occupied economy, were enormous. Britain enjoyed full employment. Additional manpower for the army and expanded defense plants would be hard to get. Some productive energy and materials would have to be diverted from consumer and export goods to arms manufacture. But, as the Chancellor of the Exchequer, Hugh Gaitskell, put it: "Our export producers are not producers of raw materials."[17] There were, however, not enough raw materials to satisfy all wants, and unfortunately for Britain the first serious cuts would occur in the most profitable and widely demanded exports, automobiles and engineering equipment. Large rearmament was bound to cut down the recovery efforts, the standard of living and the welfare services of the British Government.

Initially, the boom in the raw materials of modern war benefited Britain and the Commonwealth. Between June and December, 1950, Malayan rubber rose from 23½¢ to 71.4¢ a pound, Malayan tin from 77.8¢ to $1.46 a pound, and Australian wool from 67.8¢ to $1.13 a pound.[18] The influx of dollars into the recovering sterling area so improved the British financial position that the British Government agreed

---

[17] "If we produced all our own raw materials, no one would suggest that we stopped producing them and transferred the economic resources engaged in doing so to the sphere of defence. Obviously that would be absurd. But it would be just as absurd if we were to stop or slow down the production of exported goods." *Parliamentary Debates,* House of Commons, Vol. ??, Feb. 15, 1951, clmn.

[18] Richard M. Bissel, Jr., "The Impact of Rearmament on the Free World Economy," *Foreign Affairs* (April, 1951), 495. Prices continued to rise for most of 1951.

that after December 31, 1950, Marshall Aid to Britain should be suspended.[19] But Britain, also, had to pay these high prices, and Britain and Europe could not compete against the bidding of dollars. In December, 1950, a committee of the O.E.E.C. was sent to Washington to discuss United States-European cooperation in the purchase and allocation of raw materials. There, they were anticipated by Prime Minister Attlee, who discussed with President Truman means of increasing the supply of raw materials and their equitable distribution. This appeared to be Anglo-American association with a vengeance, and was followed by a sharp protest from Dirk Stikker at the N.A.T.O. Council meeting in Brussels.[20] By February, a cumbrous plan was worked out whereby the United States, France and Britain in association with a representative of the O.E.E.C. and producing countries and states would consider raw materials' problems in the International Materials Conference at Washington. Here, at any rate, was an occasion on which American enthusiasm for European cooperation was easily restrained.

The scale of the British armament effort, increased several times under the prodding of the United States, was, in the eyes of the British Government, dependent upon the magnitude of American financial assistance. The suspension of Marshall Aid sealed too dramatically the success of Britain's recovery. The shift from recovery to armaments and

---

[19] Britain received a total of $2,706,000,000. Britain was, also, assured that this was not a definite termination of aid. The nub of the situation was expressed in the Anglo-American communique: "The two Governments are not yet in a position to assess the ultimate economic impact of their mutual defence efforts, and the suspension of E.R.P. allotments to the United Kingdom will, in no way, affect the arrangements which are now being worked out in the North Atlantic Treaty Organization for the assessment and distribution of the burden of the defence programs of its members." *British Economic Record* (British Information Services), December 15, 1950.

[20] *Christian Science Monitor,* January 13, 1951.

Britain's need of aid for defense revealed that Britain had progressed economically but that its recovery had been neither deep nor enduring. Britain, moreover, did not receive either the amount of aid or the kind which she wanted.

Rising prices and the armaments program finally produced a public rift in the Labour leadership. In April, 1951, after the Chancellor of the Exchequer, Hugh Gaitskell, introduced charges for the National Health Service, Aneurin Bevan resigned from the Government. He did not break with the Labour Party, for his resignation represented a bold bid to gain eventually the Party leadership. He challenged the armaments program as a ruinous policy of frustrating social democracy, the true alternative to Communism. Not force, but a contented and healthy citizenry was the bulwark against revolutionary expansionism. If the arms program were reduced, Britain would be free to inaugurate a bold new program of economic development in Asia and Africa, and this would effectively sweep away the sources which made Soviet expansionism possible. Bevan's program based on very fanciful budgetary arithmetic, had great appeal for the Labour movement. It reaffirmed the flagging Socialist faith, which often appeared irrelevant in the face of Britain's limited resources. It played on Socialist hostility to armaments and suggested that a reduced arms program would be a greater surety of peace than the Government's program. Finally, a reduction of the program would enable Britain to lessen its dependence on the United States, whose succession of turbulent great debates had failed to convince the world of peaceful intent.[21]

---

[21] Bevan was correct in one respect, as Churchill later admitted. He claimed that the British Government could not carry out the arms program and could not even spend the money appropriated. Basically, however, his position appealed to those who wished to shirk the unpleasant consequences of defence preparations. The Bevanite group issued two pamphlets: *One Way*

The British Government had to be mindful of this opposition within the Labour camp and had to consider its foreign policy statements with care. The recovery of independence of action was very attractive to many British people. The mixing of British and American affairs entailed benefits but also some inconvenience and a multitude of irritations. For example, the United States pressed Britain to curtail its trade with Russia and the Satellite States. Now, while it is true that the British Government had not been vigilant about the supply of war potential to Russia, it is also true that the Soviet Union held large amounts of sterling. In return for this the Soviet Union wanted wool, rubber and machinery. From the Soviet bloc Britain secured timber, grain and bacon. Such purchases saved precious dollars. Moreover, Britain could argue that the Marshall Plan had been formulated on the expectation of the revival of trade with Eastern Europe.[22] The President of the Board of Trade, Sir Hartley Shawcross, put the British position as follows: "We should be foolish indeed to impose restrictions on our trade which weakened our own strategic position. We cannot expect sources of supply to be maintained if we do not on our side supply to these countries things which will be useful to them. . . . To deprive each part of Europe of the resources of the other will not put an end to Communism. It may merely depress the economic welfare of both parts without giving either side any relative advantage."[23]

Only and *Going Our Way;* see, also, Bevan, *In Place of Fear* (London, 1952). The inadequacy of public response to danger is powerfully analyzed in Raymond Aron, *Les Guerres en Chaine* (Paris, 1951).

[22] For a convenient summary of these trading relations, see "British Treaties with the Cominform Countries," *British Survey* (October, 1950), 28-32.

[23] Speech at Truro, Aug. 15, 1951. Text supplied by the British Information Services.

3. *The Pacific Pact and the Japanese Treaty.*

Britain's dependence on the United States was especially clear in the occupation of Japan and in the negotiation of the Japanese Peace Treaty. The United States in its position of responsibility for Japan found the demands of economic recovery there and its allies' demands for reparations incompatible. Apart from Japanese overseas assets, Britain received about $7,000,000 in industrial equipment from Japan.[24] Then in May, 1949, the United States Government terminated all reparations removals from Japan. There was some opposition in Britain, but in effect, Britain had no real voice in the Japanese occupation.[25]

Fairly early, Britain was prepared for a peace treaty with Japan. Delay in making a peace treaty arose from the Soviet insistence that the Council of Foreign Ministers should draft the major outlines of the treaty. This proposal, which would have given the Soviet Union a veto and would have excluded such countries as Australia and the Philippines from any major decision, was unacceptable to the United States and Britain. Britain favored a peace conference composed of the member states of the Far Eastern Commission with decisions to be reached by a 2/3 majority.

[24] Robert A. Fearey, *The Occupation of Japan; Second Phase: 1948-1950* (New York, 1950), pp. 143-145, 200. This equipment mainly went to Burma and Malaya.

[25] The controlling position of the United States was pointedly expressed in the following exchange in the House of Commons:

"Mr. John Paton: Is it not the case that the right of the United States Government to give interim directives refers to matters of urgency which cannot, of course, be applied to questions of this sort [termination of Japanese reparations payments], and, if that is so, by what right have the United States Government taken a unilateral decision of this kind without consultation with us?

Mr. Bevin: I would like notice of that question.

Mr. Gallacher [Communist]: He cannot answer that because it would give the game away."

Weekly Hansard, House of Commons, No. 137, Oct. 19, 1949. clmn. 536.

In September, 1949, Dean Acheson indicated that he and Bevin agreed on the urgency of a Japanese peace treaty but could not see how to proceed without Soviet participation. Later in the same year, Christopher Mayhew, Bevin's Parliamentary Secretary, said that Acheson and Bevin had argued that "the time had come to reexamine the possibilities of negotiating a peace settlement."[26] The matter was discussed at the Colombo Commonwealth Conference. Subsequently a working party of Commonwealth officials drew up a report on Commonwealth interests to be considered in such a peace treaty.

These interests ranged from Anzac fears of Japanese aggression to British fears of a revival of Japan as a commercial competitor. In general, Britain recognized that Japan had to be allowed a viable economy and considerable merchant shipping.[27] Britain asked that Japan raise her laborers' standard of living so that competition should be on more equal terms. Bevin sent a Labour Attaché to Tokyo to report on workers' conditions in Japan. Indeed, Britain favored the occupation's encouragement of effective trade unions as a means of making Japan a fairer rival. Britain increasingly recognized the necessity of Japanese trade for the development of Southeast Asia. But, on the other hand, Britain found that the dollars available for Japanese purchases caused a drain on the insufficient rice supplies which Britain sought to allocate to the areas of Southeast Asia.

When the United States determined to negotiate a treaty through ordinary diplomatic channels, the major obstacles

---

[26] *Weekly Hansard,* House of Commons, No. 141, Nov. 14, 1949, clmn. 1685.
[27] Statements by Sir Stafford Cripps, Oct. 28, 1946, *Weekly Hansard,* House of Commons, No. 30, clmns. 268-275, by Ernest Bevin, May 16, 1947, *Weekly Hansard,* House of Commons, No. 54, clmns. 1969-1970, and Christopher Mayhew, May 31, 1948, *Weekly Hansard,* House of Commons, No. 92, clmms. 617-619.

from the British side were Anzac fears of Japanese aggression and difficulties over the Chinese signatory to the peace treaty. This problem was solved by leaving China out of the peace treaty. This conclusion was reached in the course of John Foster Dulles' visits to London in June, 1950. By that time the harrowing failure of the Deputy Foreign Ministers to agree on an agenda for a meeting of the Foreign Ministers made utterly unacceptable the Soviet position that the Peace Treaty be subject to the veto of the Council of Foreign Ministers.

The anxiety of Australia and New Zealand was allayed by the Pacific Pact (Sept. 1, 1951) by which the United States, Australia and New Zealand pledged themselves to mutual defense against aggression in the Pacific area. Although it went without saying that Britain would support these Commonwealth nations in the event of war, the painful reality was that its assistance might not be adequate. The Pacific Pact was an unavoidable demonstration of the insufficiency of the Commonwealth. To those with misgivings there was cold comfort in the dutiful rejoicings that there were now still more ties between the Commonwealth and the United States.[28] After this, Britain and the Commonwealth countries (excepting India) signed the peace treaty with Japan.[29]

The Peace Treaty with Japan was accomplished by as

---

[23]   Leader in *The Times,* Sept. 3, 1951.

[29]   British writers inevitably were satirical of the American run occupation. A particularly tart viewpoint appears in Honor Tracy, *Kakemono* (London, 1950). A more restrained expression of the same approach is the following: "We no longer expect everybody to be like us and are not surprised or even vastly aggrieved when they turn out not to be. Post-Treaty Japan will prove a great disappointment to many well intentioned Americans. She should prove less of a disappointment to us, since we expect so much less of her in the way of a spiritual transformation." "A Reconditioned Japan," *The Round Table,* No. 166 (March, 1952), 126-133.

much diplomatic pageantry as the accomplishment permitted. As in Germany the settlement was not a concord of the victors but an adjustment made by some of the victors in order to win over the defeated nations to resistance against a major partner of the victorious wartime coalition. The signing of the treaty was an odd drama in which some of the most important action was taking place off stage. China and the Soviet Union were not parties to the Treaty, and to underline its inevitable inadequacies, there was the thunder of a limited war to the east.

Dependence and continued divergence of measures marked British relations with the United States in Eastern and Southeast Asia. American representatives attended a conference with the British at Colombo. The British, however, were disappointed in their hope of securing American financial participation in the Colombo Plan. The United States determined to aid such countries as India directly and not through the Colombo machinery.

4. *Extension of the Atlantic Pact to the Mediterranean.*

Thus, although Britain was associated with the United States in the Atlantic Community and derived its strength from scattered world interests, the two countries differed in their approach to important areas of the world. In one area, the Mediterranean, the problem of providing a defense organization for the southern flank of the N.A.T.O. command in Europe merged into the more perplexing problem of projecting strength into the Middle Eastern vacuum. There, while the British position was increasingly weakened, the United States, wavering between promises and inaction, achieved little coordination with Britain, and became the reluctant witness of its ally's defeat.

In considering Mediterranean defense the British were

confronted by one unit which could not readily be fitted into the Atlantic organization. Tito's Yugoslavia could not be ignored, for his defection from the Cominform provided a model which the United States and Britain sought to encourage. Britain advanced a number of small loans to Tito's government and also made several trade treaties with it. For the defense of Italy and Greece, Yugoslavia was important. But her alignment with N.A.T.O. enabled Italy to ask Britain and the United States to make good their promises (1948) of restoring Trieste to Italy. As Yugoslavia was not prepared to accept such a solution, changed circumstances confronted Britain and the United States with a painful dilemma. In Italy, a barely suppressed hostility to Britain persisted and was fostered by the failure of Britain to secure Italian trusteeship of Tripolitania and Italian Somaliland.[30]

The Mediterranean Command, under the American Admiral Carney, established in June, 1950, was primarily an attempt to protect the southern flank of Eisenhower's forces in Europe. It did not provide a general defense organization for the Mediterranean. The British hoped for a grouping of forces around their own Middle East Command in the Suez Canal area. In this policy there were several difficulties. First of all, Greece and Turkey sought membership in N.A.T.O. Britain was bound by treaty to assist those countries. But Turkey wanted the assurance of a full commitment from the United States. The Turkish Foreign Minister, Koprulu, had no confidence in the military resources of the Arab states and could see no additional strength in association with the British in Egypt. Turkey

---

[30] This arrangement was agreed to by Bevin and Count Sforza, but was defeated in the United Nations General Assembly by a combination of the Asian-Arab and Soviet states.

feared that it might become the theatre of a limited war, unlimited in destruction, however, as in Korea.[31] Although the inclusion of Turkey in N.A.T.O. did mean a great over-extension of available strength, the United States favored the Turkish request and, in September, 1951, Turkey and Greece joined N.A.T.O. Turkey's success in this matter reflected the progressive weakness of the British position in the Middle East.

On June 21, the Commonwealth Defence Ministers met in London. India, Pakistan and Ceylon did not attend, and their abstention reveals the almost tenuous laxity of the new Commonwealth's ties. Only South Africa, which had reservations about the Asiatic members of the Commonwealth and about Britain's policy of promoting self-government in African territories, was prepared to contribute seriously to Middle Eastern defence.[32] Indeed, as a British writer put it, there was so much uncertainty about even a base for defense in the Middle East that the conference would have to consider not how to defend the Middle East but how defenseless it was.[33] The resources of the Commonwealth proved to be insufficient for maintaining the British position in the Middle East.

5. *Failure in Iran.*

This weakening may be summed up in terms of the failure of Britain's effort to come to terms with Asian and Arab

---

[31]   These fears were expressed at the Council of Europe on May 14, 1951. *The Times,* June 12, 15, 1951.

[32]   The South African Prime Minister, Dr. Malan (Feb. 23, 1951) asked: "But now, as the result of the latest events and declarations of policy, the question necessarily arises—what greater solidarity or common interests or homogeneity does there exist, for example, between South Africa and Holland, or Belgium, or France, or Germany; or, for example, between Australia and the United States? Quoted in *The Round Table,* No. 163 (June, 1951), 220.

[33]   *The Observer,* June 17, 1951.

nationalism. In Iran the British Government completely failed to gauge the temper of anti-imperialist nationalism, while in the Arab world the fostering of the Arab League proved to be a boomerang.

The weird drama of Britain's eviction from Iran is a complex story in which considerable remnants of the imperialist past plagued the Labour Government. A decisive element in Iranian hostility to the British was their provocative aloofness from the Persians. They were aloof to the point of absence, and *les absents ont toujours tort*. If the British had a definite policy of emphasizing the fact that the oil concession was held by a foreigner, they could not have devised their conduct and attitudes more successfully. In the Anglo-Iranian Oil Company's settlements, the English were socially separated from the Persians, and, likewise, the whole oil area was separated from general Iranian life. It was a foreign enclave, which merely provided revenue to the government. A now conventional British argument is that the British Commonwealth is a bridge between Asia and the West but in Iran there were merely two nations held together by a cash nexus.[34] In a time of nationalism a foreign concession should have attempted to establish an organic relationship with the nation. Such an attempt was conspicuously neglected.

This lack of contact resulted in lack of understanding and the most plausible explanation of Britain's Iranian policy in 1950 and 1951 is that the British Government was not informed of the temper and conditions in Iran. Doubtless, as in Egypt, the British were accustomed to difficult times

---

[34] There is a good analysis of the attitudes which produced "forever England" in this corner of a foreign land in "Cause and Effect in Persia," *The World Today*, VII (August, 1951), 329-338. A sharper tone is sounded in an article by a former employee of the Company, James Callow, "Company Funeral?", *The Spectator*, CLXXXVI (May 25, 1951), 680.

and poisonous suspicions. They probably thought that this was a "time of troubles" such as they had weathered in 1933. In the past the British Government has been able to think that if one Persian government proved troublesome, a new and more agreeable one would soon appear. In the ensuing nationalization crisis, they did not recognize the fact that the nationalist temper had created a new situation. Agreement was impossible, because agreement meant a sell-out for the nationalist cause. A dictator could not have helped the British, because a dictator would have had to be nationalist. Against agreement stood a long-standing Persian mistrust. The Persians had credited Britain with a fabulous power of devious intrigue.[35] This reputation was a source of strength when Britain was powerful. But it served to make her more hateful after her weakness was revealed in India and Palestine. Mistrust of such an order made responsible bargaining very difficult.

When the Majlis rejected the Soviet Oil Concession in 1947, the Iranian nationalists had tasted blood. American support of Iran may also have suggested that in the Iranian attack on the British concession the United States might serve as a protector of anti-imperialism. At any rate, the initial request for a greater return to the Iranian Government from the concession was not immoderate. The world demand for oil had caused favorable terms to be granted to Venezuela and, later, to the Arab neighbors of Iran.

The Anglo-Iranian Oil Company's contract regulated payments to the Government in proportion to the Company's dividend payments. There was an element of generosity in this procedure, for the dividends were based on the

---

[35] T. Cuyler Young, "The National and International Relations of Iran," in *Near Eastern Culture and Society*, edited by T. Cuyler Young (Princeton, 1951), pp. 193-194.

world-wide activities of the Company. The British Government, however, had limited dividend payments of all British companies. The contract was exceedingly complicated, and the supplemental agreement negotiated in July, 1949, was even more complicated.[36] This in itself was a difficulty. It was easy for the nationalists to argue that the British government took a larger sum of money from the Company in taxes than the Iranian Government received for the concession. Moreover, it was easy to understand that the British Government owned a majority of the Company's stock.[37] The details of the contract were not only complicated, but they were not publicized in Persia. Indeed, the Company announced that it was up to the Persians to make publicity for the agreement.[38] This unbelievable attitude was doubtless taken on the advice of the Old Persian Hands, who represented the Government on the Anglo-Iranian Board of Directors. As they were from the Treasury, they were primarily interested in revenue, and their knowledge of Persia dated from the palmy days of empire.

No action was taken by the Iranian Majlis for almost eighteen months. During this extraordinarily long period of

---

[36] Iran's overall financial returns from the Anglo-Iranian Oil Company's activities are well summarized in a letter to the *Manchester Guardian,* June 30, 1951. In an otherwise excellent article, Ambassador Grady does not do justice to the Company's financial offer. "What Went Wrong in Iran?", *Saturday Evening Post,* Jan. 5, 1952.

[37] Dr. Mossadegh, then chairman of the Majlis Oil Committee, gave a characteristically simplified and distorted account of Iran's returns from the Oil Company on Oct. 19, 1950. It is quoted in Lewis V. Thomas and Richard N. Frye, *The United States and Turkey and Iran* (Cambridge, 1951), pp. 255-256. Useful material on Anglo-Iranian financial matters may be found in Angus Sinclair, "Iranian Oil," *Middle Eastern Affairs,* II (June, 1951), 213-224.

[38] "Cause and Effect in Persia," *The World Today,* VII (August, 1951), 334. The British note to the Iranian Government (March 14, 1951) complained that the Majlis discussed the agreement irrelevantly and that the details of the agreement were never explained to the Iranian public.

delay it became apparent that the supplementary agreement was political poison in Iran. But foreigners found it difficult to regard the Majlis as a serious legislature. It was corrupt and appeared incapable of reform. The Iranian administration was not much better. Elaborate plans for the economic development of Iran, the Seven-Year Plan devised by a group of foreign specialists, the Overseas Consultants, Inc., were eroded away. Finally, early in 1951, the contracts of these foreign specialists were cancelled. The ambitious Plan, which was to have been financed from oil revenues, would have required new taxation, and the Majlis wanted no such burden.

The Plan was also based on expectations of United States Aid. The sending of Henry F. Grady as Ambassador to Iran appeared to be an indication that such aid would be forthcoming, for Grady had acquired a reputation for his administration of American aid to Greece. Yet, no substantial aid arrived. Then the Iranian Government indulged in an old game, playing one enemy against another. It concluded a trade treaty with the Soviet Union. This ended the practical quarantine of Soviet officials in Iran and failed to provide that Soviet trade agents deal only with officials of Iranian Government trading companies. Shortly afterwards relays of Voice of America broadcasts were banned in Iran. Bahram Shahrukh, Director General of Propaganda, explained: "The Iranian Government has not much patience with America, for Iran has received only $5,000,000, some obsolete machinery and unwanted technicians."[39]

The year 1950, the decisive year, was lost in futile efforts to persuade the Majlis to accept the supplementary agreement. When Ali Mansur's government fell in June, 1950, it should have been clear that some new terms had

---

[39] *The Observer,* Nov. 19, 1950.

to be offered. His successor, Prime Minister Ali Razmara, finally withdrew it from the Majlis six months later. To suggestions that new concessions be made, the Oil Company had originally replied that it waited the acceptance or rejection of the supplementary agreement. Ali Razmara insisted that the Persians could not operate the Company but the Majlis, sparked on by a small faction, the National Front of Doctor Mossadegh, clamored for nationalization as the cure for all Iran's ills. This demand was supported by religious groups and one of their number assassinated Ali Razmara on March 7, 1951. For a few days there was an understandable reluctance of poltical leaders to succeed the dead Prime Minister. Hussein Ala, who had sought American assistance against the Soviet Union in 1946, became Prime Minister, and the Majlis on March 15 voted to nationalize the oil fields.

Until April 29, when Doctor Mossadegh became Prime Minister, there may have been some chance of remedial action. During this period, however, the British Government limited itself to protests against the nationalization law as an act of expropriation and as a violation of contract. An offer of a fifty-fifty share of the profits to the Iranian Government, made earlier, had become obsolete. But Hussein Ala and the Shah recognized that Iran could not operate the oil business and hoped for some accommodation. The British Government, unfortunately, did not act and Hussein Ala's moderation was paralyzed by nationalist charges that the "oil company has reserved him for twenty years to bring him to power at the present time."[40] He resigned on April 27, 1951.

Two days later, Doctor Mossadegh came to power. His

---

[40] Deputy Reza Ashtianizedeh in the Majlis, *New York Times,* April 9, 1951.

National Front consisted of a few deputies who were mainly elected from Teheran and expressed the wild and irrepressible nationalism of the urban groups, the clerks, workers, journalists, lawyers and mullahs, the very people whom the British never knew. This incorruptible Robespierre had simplified all problems to one problem, the ejection of the Oil Company from Iran. Foreign technicians might be necessary, but he insisted that their status would have to be that of employees of the Iranian Government. Other and practical considerations concerned him not at all.[41]

All the traditional gambits of British policy, the intervention of the Shah, tribal rebellion, or the creation of a new Government, were nullified by the nationalistic temper. Thereafter, the British Government sought to deal with Mossadegh as a reasonable blackmailer who eventually would have to come to terms.[42] Vainly, he was read a lesson in economics. Iran did not have its own technicians, and, above all, it had no tankers. The Company's world-wide distribution system was run from London. British technicians

---

41 The subsequent policy of the British Government was not based on such a reading of Mossadegh's character. Yet such knowledge was not lacking in England, as appears in the following excerpt from a "profile" sketch in *The Observer*, May 20, 1951. "British negotiators should have the perception to understand that Moussadek is wholly impervious to common sense arguments of expediency. In spite of their long and bitter experience of nationalists, it seems impossible for the British to realise that Moussadek would rather Persian oil ran into the sea . . . than that foreigners should continue to exploit it. Although he may speciously claim that the expropriation of the Company would bring benefits to the poor of Persia, he is really quite indifferent to its results. The expropriation is an end in itself." This analysis is wonderfully supported by a reported conversation between W. Averell Harriman and Mossadegh in Joseph and Stewart Alsop, "Must We Surrender the Middle East?", *Saturday Evening Post*, April 12, 1952.

42 M. A. Fitzsimons, "Crisis in Iran," *The Commonweal*, LIV (August 3, 1951), 399-400. Ambassador Grady wrote: "The concept that financial pressures would bring the Iranians into line and solve the oil problem in Iran was from the beginning the key to the British blunders."

would refuse to work under direct Persian management, for skilled workers required a considerable inducement in pay and pleasant conditions of work to live in the heat and ugliness of the oil-fields. The lesson was stretched out through June as the refineries came to a stop. Abadan became a dead loss, the government was losing money, and Dr. Mossadegh still did not relent in the face of the persuasions of President Truman's representative, W. Averell Harriman, and of the offers of the British negotiator, Richard Stokes.

The British Government appealed to the International Court of Justice and secured an injunction, which the Iranian Government disregarded. The apparently imminent loss of the Oil Company roused bitter debate in the British Parliament. Foreign Secretary Morrison was unable to do more than present a historical account of British Middle Eastern policy to the House of Commons. Labour Ministers regularly insisted that the Government would protect the lives of British subjects, but never said that it would protect British property.[43] On one occasion Prime Minister Attlee did say that the British would not leave Abadan. Actually all the British technicians were withdrawn in early October. Opening the Conservative election campaign at Liverpool, Mr. Churchill made the serious charge that Dr. Mossadegh had "penetrated and measured accurately the will power of the men he had to deal with in Whitehall."[44] The consequence was the loss of the largest oil refineries in the world,

---

[43] Ambassador Grady said that strong American representations were required to prevent the British from forcible intervention. This statement may be based on British talk in Iran, rather than on any decision of the British cabinet.

[44] *The Manchester Guardian Weekly*, Oct. 4, 1951. As the British failure was based on the failure of British diplomats and businessmen to understand developments in Iran, it is interesting to speculate on what Mr. Churchill would have done. He suggested no alternatives during or after the crisis.

thirty million tons of oil yearly and Britain's most profitable overseas investment.

The Iranian affair had immediate repercussions in Iraq. The Iraqui Prime Minister, Nuri-es-Said Pasha, opposed demands for the nationalization of the Iraq Petroleum Company on the grounds that the state already owned the oilfields and merely leased them to the Company. The Company quickly came to terms with the Government on an offer of a fifty-fifty division of the profits.

But the British position in the Arab world was rapidly deteriorating. The Arab defeat in the Israeli war remained a perpetual sore. This defeat revealed the weakness of the Arab League, which the British had originally fostered. The League was held together as much by the antagonisms of the Arab states as by the desire for Arab unity. The British were charged not only with the sins of imperialism but with support of Israel. When Britain's aptest Arab pupil, Abdullah, incorporated Arab Palestine into his territory, the other Arab states, excepting Iraq, threatened Jordan. Abdullah sought to make a peace treaty with Israel, but even he was finally deterred from making peace. On July 20, 1951, this astute man, the only staunch Arab ally of the British, was assassinated.[45]

6. *Egypt Tears Up the Treaty of 1936.*

In Egypt the stalemate of 1947 continued and grew more irritating. To have held a controlling influence on Egypt and the Arab League Britain would have required something to offer, for example, financial aid for development. Instead, Britain was a debtor to Egypt. A financial agreement of 1947, which provided that a part of the sterling balances

---

[45] For details, see *The Times,* July 26, 1951, and an absorbing article, "King Abdullah's Assassins," *The World Today,* VII (October, 1951).

each year should be freely convertible, was cancelled after the convertibility crisis of 1947.[46] This was particularly damaging to Britain's financial and moral credit in Egypt.

When Britain abdicated in Palestine and the Arab states were defeated, she began to recognize that the Arab League was useless to her. Egypt tried to use the League against Britain and efforts to stabilize the area after the war.[47] In 1949 the British agreed to supply Egypt with tanks and jet-aircraft. But the Egyptian Government, now in the hands of the Wafd Party, continued its nationalist demands for the evacuation of the Canal Zone and the unity of the Nile Valley. It also banned oil shipments through the Canal to the Haifa refinery in Israel, already denied oil from the Iraq pipeline. This boycott was expensive and humiliating for Britain. Conservative Party members often insisted that this kowtow would be fatal in the Middle East. In October, 1950, the British Government, yielding to Conservative and Labour critics suspended shipments of tanks and planes to Egypt. The Egyptians branded this action as evidence of Britain's determination to keep Egypt incapable of defending the Canal.

But this suspension followed an announcement in the speech from the Egyptian throne to the Parliament that the Treaty of 1936 would be annulled. One further effort to secure a solution took place in April, 1951. The British Government offered to evacuate the Canal Zone within five years. To protect this area a joint Anglo-Egyptian Air defense plan would be drawn up. This proposal provided for

---

[46] Sir Frederick Leith-Ross, "Financial and Economic Developments in Egypt," *International Affairs*, XXVIII (January, 1952), 29-33.

[47] Two valuable articles on this subject are "The Arab League: Development and Difficulties," *The World Today*, VII (May, 1951), 187-196, and Esmond Wright, "The "Greater Syria" Project in Arab Politics," *World Affairs* (July, 1951).

measures which many Egyptians and Arabs recognized to be necessary. General Fuad Sadek, Commander in Chief of Egyptian forces in Palestine had said: "I am and shall remain all my life an Egyptian hostile to imperialism, under which I suffered much. Nevertheless, I say quite frankly that a joint defense with Britain is absolutely necessary in the existing circumstance, but with certain reservations."[48]

The British offer was curtly rejected. The reasons for the rejection are to be sought not in the inadequacies of the proposal but in the internal politics of Egypt. The Wafd Party had created such a nationalist temper in the city mobs of Egypt that its leaders had become the prisoners of their agitation. The failure of the Wafd to achieve even a measure of social progress and the extraordinary corruption of its administration compelled it to maintain the nationalist struggle on a feverish level in order to keep other parties or groups from making inroads into the ranks of the Wafd. Two other difficulties, also, prevented any compromise or bargain. Arrangements for regional defense demanded a peace settlement with Israel. Although Sidky Pasha had favored peace with Israel, he was a very lonely voice. The prevailing temper in the Arab League is revealed in an attack on the Syrian Prime Minister Kudsi for being silent on his defense plans. He was then accused of planning to enter an alliance which would include Israel. Peace with Israel, the opponent said, was treason to Syria. The Prime Minister replied that no Syrian would dare to dream of peace with Israel.[49]

Perhaps even more decisive was the fact that the Egyptians sensed the weakness of Britain and especially the reluc-

---

[43] *New York Times,* Aug. 28, 1950.
[49] *New York Times,* Dec. 22, 1950.

tance of the Labour Government to use force to maintain positions. So many Labour Party speakers in 1946 had urged the surrender of British positions in Egypt that Egyptian nationalists were convinced of the imminence of victory for their national cause. It became a commonplace of the more serious Egyptian press to suggest, as *Al Ahram* did, that the Labour Government's firmness towards Egypt was caused by their fear of the Conservatives.[50]

This belief was fortified by British actions in Iran, and the British protest to the Security Council against the Egyptian blockade of oil to Israel through the Suez Canal only intensified Egyptian anger.[51]

By this time bargaining and diplomacy had become futile. As the Wafdist President of the Chamber of Deputies put the position: "So far as we are concerned, we want no new treaty. We just want to abrogate the 1936 treaty."[52] A non-committal and long-suffering remark of Herbert Morrison (July 30) was interpreted by the Egyptian Foreign Minister as a closing of the door to further negotiations.

In September, the Egyptian Government was informed of proposals that Egypt, Turkey, France, Britain and the United States should establish a Middle East Command in the Suez Canal area. The Wafd leaders finally pushed through legislation (Oct. 15, 1951) which unilaterally abro-

---

[50] *The Times*, Nov. 22, 1950.

[51] All the political articles and leaders in *The Sunday Times* and *The Observer*, June 24, 1951, stressed Britain's lack of force and the lack of will in the Labour Government.

[52] *New York Times*, April 14, 1951. Charles Malik of Lebanon expressed his diplomatic doubts and his Christian hope about a solution in a very important article. He hoped that a working formula "embodying the essential interests and rights of all concerned can be found. Not to believe in this is to worship utter darkness: to despair of the power of man, coming back to himself with a purified heart, to rise above and reconcile conflicting interests." "The Near East: the Search for Truth," *Foreign Affairs* (January, 1952), 235.

gated the Treaty of 1936 and proclaimed Farouk as king of the Sudan.[53]

Short of war, this was as far as the Egyptian Government could go. When Egyptian labor was withdrawn from the bases, and the Government encouraged forms of guerilla warfare, the usefulness of the bases was greatly reduced.

This new defiance of Britain occurred during the parliamentary elections. In the campaign the Labour Party refurbished its charge of Tory war-mongering, and used its failures in Iran and Egypt as evidence that a steady and peacefully inclined hand was on the trigger of British rearmament.[54] As a preliminary to the elections, the dissident factions of the Labour Party joined in a wholehearted crusade against the Tories and the danger of war.

7. *Defeat of the Labour Government: Conclusion.*

The Labour attack on Winston Churchill as a warmonger stung the Conservative leader. Churchill may once have entertained the hope that the American superiority in atomic weapons might be used as a threat to force the Soviet Union to a final showdown. Later developments, revealing the formidable character of Soviet power and position, dampened that hope.

After Labour's defeat, Churchill, as Prime Minister, got his revenge. The revenge took the form of revealing Labour's Secretary, Herbert Morrison, as the dupe of his own electoral slogans, and of a dramatic demonstration of the Con-

---

[53] In defending Labour's policy in Iran, Labour speakers effectively reassured Egypt. Ernest Davies, Labour's Parliamentary Under-Secretary for Foreign Affairs, said: "Because wrong methods are used and the rule of law set aside, there is no justification for resorting to force to insist on the maintenance of rights in the territories of foreign powers, which wish to terminate those rights." *The Times*, Oct. 12, 1951.

[54] M. A. Fitzsimons, "The British Elections," *The Review of Politics*, XIV (January, 1952), 102-120.

tinuity of British Foreign Policy. Churchill in speaking to the United States Congress had vaguely pledged that Britain would join the United States in prompt and effective action against Chinese infractions of any future truce agreement. The Labour Party used this as the occasion for a motion of censure against Churchill for having failed in his American visit to give adequate expression to Britain's policy on China and Korea.

Churchill's reply (Feb. 27, 1952) reported that the Labour Government had in May and September, 1951, agreed to actions against China, commitments which would have widened the War. "I had no wish or need to proclaim any new policy to Congress because, so far as policy is concerned, in Korea and China, we were only following in accord with our own convictions the policy entered into and long pursued by our predecessors."[55] Earlier in the speech he paid tribute to the late Ernest Bevin for carrying out the policy outlined in Churchill's Fulton Speech.[56]

This debate painfully disclosed Labour's lack of adroitness in foreign affairs. It was, indeed, true that the foreign policy of the Labour Government was Churchillian in its major lines. Yet circumstances and British interests, and not the inspiration of Churchill, dictated the policy. The policy sought to protect British world-wide interests by keeping the Soviet Union out of the Mediterranean, by adjusting Britain's position in the Middle East and Asia to the anti-imperialist temper of the post-war period. The necessity of adjustment was perceived but in Iran and Egypt was not successfully implemented.

When it appeared that cooperation with the Soviet Un-

---

[55] *United States News and World Report,* March 7, 1952, 90.

[56] This continuity of policy is strikingly revealed in similar speeches, delivered on March 31, 1952, by Attlee and Foreign Secretary Eden.

ion was impossible on any terms but surrender to Soviet expansionism, the British Labour Government joined in the cooperative recovery effort sponsored by the United States. In the movement towards European Unity the Labour Government refused to merge Britain in Europe, for while Britain is geographically on the ocean flank of Europe, it has also used the ocean to create overseas a multitude of ties and interests, essential to Britain's survival and security. Labour and Conservative Parties are at one in stressing these non-European links.

Later, the Labour Government supported the defense of Europe by promoting the Brussels Treaty and North Atlantic Treaties. The defensive character of these treaties was emphasized, but these efforts to create strength were power politics. Security of the Kingdom took priority over even social welfare politics. Many members of the Labour Party did not like this emphasis on the grim necessity of power. Some, like Aneurin Bevan, suggested that power was not the effective reply to power. But the Labour leaders accepted the implications of defense.

The question of a Socialist foreign policy arose only to become absurd. The continuity of British foreign policy prevailed because British interests remained the same and the suspicion of state for state survived.

In seeking strength for survival Britain could not have recourse to the balance-of-power policy. There were but two big powers, and Britain could not mediate between them. There was no alternative but alliance with Western Europe and the United States. Conservative and Labour leaders were agreed on all these issues. Indeed, it is difficult to find a major issue of policy on which they disagreed. Britain could not have held India, though Mr. Churchill, out of office, was opposed to a policy of "scuttle;" as a respon-

179

sible Minister, however, he would have had to recognize the necessity of withdrawing in India. The only difference was that Labour's traditions favored independence for the Empire, whereas Churchill criticized Labour's surrender of Empire, without suggesting alternatives, except that now and then, he was able enough to disguise British weakness and to keep Asian and African nationalists from reading his mind.

---

[57] After my book had been submitted to the printers, Stanford Press published *British Labour's Foreign Policy* by Professor Elaine Windrich. Her conclusion, directly opposed to mine, is that the Labour Government maintained not a continuity of British foreign policy but a continuity in the aims and principles of the Labour Party's foreign policy program. This utter disagreement may partly be explained by the author's almost exclusive concentration on the statements of principles by the Labour leaders and in the Labour Party's publications. This abstract approach is readily victimized by the generalities of policy statements. As foreign policy is formulated to advance particular interests and to meet specific situations, I have attempted a concrete approach. Even Professor Windrich recognizes the vagueness of the slogan "a Socialist Foreign Policy."

INDEX

PRINTED AT AVE MARIA PRESS

DATE DUE

AP 13 '78			
FE 9 79			
AP2 '80			
AP 2 '80			
GAYLORD			PRINTED IN U.S.A.